Favorite Problems

Dale Seymour

DALE SEYMOUR PUBLICATIONS
P.O. BOX 10888
PALO ALTO, CA 94303

Dedicated to the memory of Susan Pfingstel, employee and friend.

Production Coordinator: Ruth Cottrell
Illustrator: Rob Browne
Cover Art: Julie Peterson

ISBN 0-86651-085-0

Order Number DSO1234

12 13 14 15 16 17-MA-95

DALE
SEYMOUR
PUBLICATIONS
P.O. BOX 10888
PALO ALTO, CA 94303

CONTENTS

INTRODUCTION

Favorite Problems is a collection of 16 sets of classical problems for grades 5–7. Each set of three related problems includes a Warm-up problem, an illustrated Poster problem, and an Extension problem. Available separately are the 16 Poster problems, spiral-bound in a calendar-style format, with motivating illustrations in vibrant color for use as classroom posters.

Reproducible worksheets for students

Each of the 48 different problems appears on a separate page with space allowed for students to write their solutions or other notes. Duplicate the pages, and either hand out the problems one at a time, give them as in-class work, or assign them for homework.

Discussions for the teacher

On the back of each student worksheet page is a discussion of the problem including the answer, a detailed solution, hints to help the students get started, background information on the problem, specific teaching suggestions, and ways to extend the problem.

Problem sequence

There is no required order for using the 16 sets of problems. Simply choose those sets that best suit your students' learning situation. But within each set of problems, it is best to assign the Warm-up problem first, then the Poster problem, and finally the Extension problem. It is *not* necessary to use all 48 problems. Sometimes you may use a week or more in worthwhile discussion of a single problem, taking the time to carry that discussion to its fullest.

Focus on problem solving

These problems have been chosen to help you concentrate on the development of students' problem-solving skills rather than on algebraic or geometric structure. Most of the solutions require only the use of basic arithmetic. They may, of course, be solved using some algebra or geometry. Students will be able to use the mathematical skills they already have.

Problem-solving strategies

The problems themselves can be solved in more than one way and different problems require different strategies. Some of the strategies that students will find helpful are these:

Look for a pattern.
Guess and check.
Write an equation.
Use logical reasoning.
Work backwards.
Draw a picture.
Make an organized list.
Make a table.
Make a tree diagram.
Use objects or act out the problem.
Solve a simpler related problem.

Suggestions for teaching problem solving.

Problem solving should be a part of every student's daily work. One way is to provide from ten to fifteen minutes of *each* class period for discussion and work on problems. Very few problems are completed in a single period, but this gives students time to digest the problems, think about them, leave them alone, and come back with new, fresh ideas. Make each class like the *Perils of Pauline,* right down to the last minute. That's when you give a good question to ponder, one that students can't quite get out of their minds.

Here are some suggestions that are essential for anyone who is planning to teach problem solving.

Work the problems.

Before assigning a problem to your class, work it yourself. You will have a much better feeling for the problem and be able to anticipate difficulties that students may encounter.

Define the problems.

Carefully discuss the intent of a new problem when you introduce it. Read the problem along with the class and invite questions. Taking care that students understand a problem is essential to their success.

Require records of work.

Encourage students to keep a record of their work on a problem. Students should record all attempts, failures as well as successes. They should give explanations of their thinking. Such records are helpful for later reference and as a needed ingredient for research.

Allow students to devise their own plans.

Different approaches are possible, depending on the insights and skills of each student. Discussions of different ways of looking at a problem are very illuminating to both class and teacher alike.

Look for simpler related problems.

Urge students to look for simpler problems that give insights into the problem at hand. For example ask, "What's the simplest problem? Don't bother with the hard stuff at first." Often a simpler problem provides the key to a solution.

Generalize.

When students are capable of generalizing, ask for generalizations, but don't expect rigid, formal statements. In many cases, students will have a feeling for the solution to a problem, but will be unable to completely formalize it. Help them out.

Take time.

Carry discussions to their fullest. Give students the chance to work with a problem and play around with it until something "pops."

Answer questions with questions.

Don't give free information. Students must learn to think and reason through solutions themselves.

Look back at what has been done.

How was the problem solved? Is there another way? Does this look like the solution to any other problem? Does it suggest other problems for investigation?

Be actively involved with a problem.

You can't teach problem solving unless you are involved with it yourself. Work the problems on your own. What are possible approaches? What difficulties will students have? How does it tie into other work students have had? What new problems does it suggest?

Solving a problem may not be fun so much as it is hard work. But the pleasure in reaching a successful solution makes the effort worthwhile.

A DISCOVERY LESSON

The discovery teaching technique is perhaps the best way to present difficult problems to young students. Through a sequence of questions, observations, and hints, you can help the students to participate in the discovery of a solution. The more actively involved the students are with the process of finding a solution, the more meaning the problem-solving activity will have for them.

The author has chosen a particularly rich and interesting problem with which to demonstrate the following discovery lesson, problem 8. *Extension.*

> Discover the rule for finding the number of different rectangles in a square grid containing *c* columns and *r* rows.

This is a good problem, so we will work this one together as a class. First, let's make sure we understand the problem. (Have someone restate it.) We want to find a rule or formula that will allow us to find the total number of rectangles in *any* grid of squares.

For example, in this 5 by 5 grid we are looking for all the rectangles.

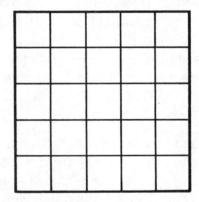

What is a rectangle? (A four-sided polygon with four right angles.)

Is a square a rectangle? (Yes.) Okay, then we will want to count all the squares.

What is the largest rectangle in the 5 by 5 grid? (The outside or perimeter of the grid.)

What is meant by *different* rectangles? Different size? Different shape? Different position? The problem doesn't make that clear. When a problem can be interpreted differently or the exact meaning isn't clear, we say the problem is *ambiguous*. This problem is slightly ambiguous. *I think* what the problem means is that two rectangles are different if they don't have the same four vertices (corners). So each of the small squares will be counted as different rectangles.

Any other questions about what the problem is asking before we begin? (What do you mean by finding a rule?) Finding a rule means to find a formula that will quickly solve this problem for any size grid such as the rule we have for finding the area of a rectangle. We express that rule in words by saying the area of a rectangle is given by its length times its width. We express the formula in symbols by $A = l \times w$. This is the kind of rule we are looking for.

Let's get back to our 5 by 5 grid. How many rectangles do you think are in this figure? Wait! Before you start trying to count them, let's make an estimate. Not an estimate as to what the rule will be, but an estimate as to how many different rectangles there are in a 5 by 5 grid. Think about it briefly. Now make your best guess. Don't worry about being wrong; just see how close you are when we find the answer. Skill in estimation is developed only by practice. Write your answer some place where you can come back and check it later.

We've never looked for a rule before. How do we go about this? Does anybody have any ideas? (Probably silence.) Well, let's say that we found the number of different rectangles in the 5 by 5 grid. How would that help? (If we found that number, maybe it would relate to the numbers 5 and 5 in some way that would give us a clue.) Good thinking! Are there lots of rectangles in the 5 by 5 grid? (Yes.) Too many to count? (No, but it would be hard.) Will the rule we are looking for give us the answer to a 50 by 100 grid? (Hopefully, yes.) It should. Will it give us the answer to a 2 by 3 grid? (Yes.) Which would you rather count — the number of different rectangles in a 2 by 3 grid, a 5 by 5 grid or a 50 by 100 grid? (A 2 by 3 grid.) A 2 by 3 grid, of course! Okay, why don't we start there.

Sketch a 2 by 3 grid on a piece of scratch paper, and let's take a few minutes to see how many different rectangles you count. (This takes about two minutes.) Let's see what you counted. How many did you get? Jane? (16) Okay. Did anyone get a different answer? Sue? (18) Okay. Any other answers? (15) Wait a minute! Shouldn't there be just one answer? Some of you either missed some rectangles or counted them twice. If we can't count accurately on a 2 by 3 grid, think of the problem we might have had with the 5 by 5 or 50 by 100 grid. How many got 16 for the answer? (Three hands.) How many got 15? (One hand and a red face.) How many got 18? (Three-fourths of the class.) Well, it looks like 18 is the most popular answer at least. Will someone who got 18 tell me how they counted? Joe. (First I counted the six little squares.

Then I counted the one-by-two rectangles and there were four of those.)

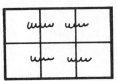

Excuse me, Joe. That's a good start but how did you know to refer to the larger rectangles as one-by-twos? (I don't know. I had to call them something!) That's good, Joe. You picked a good name. Let's call them one-by-twos. Continue, Joe. (There were two of these one-by-threes and three one-by-twos going the other way.) Excuse me again, Joe. It may be important to stop here for a minute and have us all agree upon some wording so that we are sure we are all talking about the same thing. Instead of saying one-by-twos this way and one-by-twos that way, let's agree on a way. Let's call these two-by-ones.

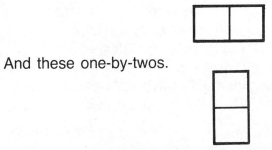

And these one-by-twos.

We count to the right first and then up. Just like when we plot points on a grid. That will help us remember. It could be important because we see in this problem we counted four two-by-ones and only three one-by-twos. Let's write two-by-one as 2×1. When you go to the lumber store, how do you ask for lumber? (Two by fours.) How is it written? (2×4) Okay, back to Joe.

Sorry for the interruption, Joe, but you came up with a good system. We just had to be sure it had no *ambiguities.* Let's make a list of your counting on the board. We started with a 3 by 2 grid. How many 1×1 rectangles? (6) How many 2×1? (4) How many 3×1? (2) How many 4×1? (None.) Good! How many 1×2? (3) What is left? (2×2 rectangles. There are 2 of them!) Good, Bill! Anything else? (The whole figure.) Okay, what is it? (A 2×3.) Is that right, class? (No, it's a 3×2. You count right first.) Okay. Let's see, that gives us a total of ... 18. Eighteen was right.

$1 \times 1 \longrightarrow 6$
$2 \times 1 \longrightarrow 4$
$3 \times 1 \longrightarrow 2$
$1 \times 2 \longrightarrow 3$
$2 \times 2 \longrightarrow 2$
$3 \times 2 \longrightarrow 1$

Total: 18

Now that we have an answer, 18, how does that help us? We are looking for a rule that relates 2 and 3 to 18. Any ideas? (Lengthy silence.) Come on — try anything. Jane. (Well, $2 \times 3^2 = 18$.) Good. There is a relationship. It may be our rule. The number of rows times the number of columns squared, 2×3^2, certainly does equal 18.

What do we do with our guessed rule? How do we know if it will work on all examples? (Silence.) Come on, we need some ideas. What do we do next? (Try it on another grid.) Great idea! The problem-solving technique we're using now is called guess and test. We've guessed a rule; let's test it. What will we test it on? (Silence — finally, on the 5 by 5 grid?) Okay. If we were to test it on the 5 by 5 grid, the answer might be what? (Silence — finally, 5 times 5^2.) Okay. 5×5^2 is 125. Are there 125 rectangles in the 5 by 5 grid? We don't know; we haven't counted them yet. We could do that, but what might be easier? (Test it on a simpler grid, like 2 by 2.) Good idea. It is easier to count the rectangles in a 2 by 2 grid than a 5 by 5 grid.

Draw a 2 by 2 grid on your scratch paper and count the different rectangles. How many did you get? (9) How many got 9? Good. Okay, we are testing a rule: one number times the other squared gives the total. Does it work here? (No.) Why not? (Because $2 \times 2^2 = 8$, not 9.) The rule we are looking for must work on *all* cases not just one. Have we found our rule yet? (No.) Back to the drawing board!

I know what you're thinking. You're thinking this problem is too hard for you. Well, you're wrong! I'll tell you there is a relationship between 2, 3 and 18 that *is* the answer. When you see it, you will say, 'Why didn't I think of that!' Let's keep looking, and we'll find it! Any other ideas besides $2 \times 3^2 = 18$? (Silence.) Okay, then I'm going to have to give you a little hint. The key to unlocking the problem is through seeing a *pattern.* Looking for patterns in mathematics is important. Many people have described mathematics as the study of pattern. Let's try another example and see if we observe a pattern that reveals the rule to us. We are going to draw a 4 by 3 grid here on the board. Four columns and three rows. Now we will find the number of different rectangles in this figure by making a complete listing of each type of rectangle, 1×1, 1×2, and so on.

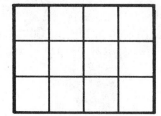

$1 \times 1 \rightarrow 12$
$1 \times 2 \rightarrow 8$
$1 \times 3 \rightarrow ?$

What pattern is developing? Without counting the 1 × 3 rectangles, can you guess what the answer might be? (4) Right. Four fits the pattern. Now count to see if there are, in fact, four 1 × 3 rectangles. (There are!) Let's continue our listing. How many 2 × 1 rectangles? (9) How many 2 × 2? (6) Without counting, the pattern might reveal how many 2 × 3 rectangles. Count them. (There are 3.)

$$1 \times 1 \to 12 \qquad 2 \times 1 \to 9$$
$$1 \times 2 \to 8 \qquad 2 \times 2 \to 6$$
$$1 \times 3 \to 4 \qquad 2 \times 3 \to ?$$

Let's look for a pattern to complete our list without counting. Then we'll check to see if our guesses were right.

$$1 \times 1 \to 12 \qquad 2 \times 1 \to 9 \qquad 3 \times 1 \to 6 \qquad 4 \times 1 \to \_$$
$$1 \times 2 \to 8 \qquad 2 \times 2 \to 6 \qquad 3 \times 2 \to \_ \qquad 4 \times 2 \to \_$$
$$1 \times 3 \to 4 \qquad 2 \times 3 \to 3 \qquad 3 \times 3 \to \_ \qquad 4 \times 3 \to \_$$

The final listing gives us

$$1 \times 1 \to 12 \qquad 2 \times 1 \to 9 \qquad 3 \times 1 \to 6 \qquad 4 \times 1 \to 3$$
$$1 \times 2 \to 8 \qquad 2 \times 2 \to 6 \qquad 3 \times 2 \to 4 \qquad 4 \times 2 \to 2$$
$$1 \times 3 \to 4 \qquad 2 \times 3 \to 3 \qquad 3 \times 3 \to 2 \qquad 4 \times 3 \to 1$$

The total number of rectangles is 60. Now once again we ask the question, 'In a 4 by 3 grid, how do 4 and 3 relate to 60?' (The class is usually silent.) It isn't obvious, but remember my hint, we were looking for a pattern. Let's go back and look at the patterns that developed in the problem.

Using one column: 12 + 8 + 4 (multiples of ?)
Using two columns: 9 + 6 + 3 (multiples of ?)
Using three columns: 6 + 4 + 2 (multiples of ?)
Using four columns: 3 + 2 + 1 (multiples of ?)

We could write these as:

$$12 + 8 + 4 = 4 \times 3 + 4 \times 2 + 4 \times 1$$
$$9 + 6 + 3 = 3 \times 3 + 3 \times 2 + 3 \times 1$$
$$6 + 4 + 2 = 2 \times 3 + 2 \times 2 + 2 \times 1$$
$$3 + 2 + 1 = 1 \times 3 + 1 \times 2 + 1 \times 1$$

We see some patterns. Using the distributive property, we could re-write these sums. (This may need more explanation depending on the level of the students.)

$$4 \times 3 + 4 \times 2 + 4 \times 1 = 4(3 + 2 + 1)$$
$$3 \times 3 + 3 \times 2 + 3 \times 1 = 3(3 + 2 + 1)$$
$$2 \times 3 + 2 \times 2 + 2 \times 1 = 2(3 + 2 + 1)$$
$$1 \times 3 + 1 \times 2 + 1 \times 1 = 1(3 + 2 + 1)$$

What factor does each expression have in common? $(3 + 2 + 1)$
Instead of writing the final sum of 60, let's write the sum this way:

$4(3 + 2 + 1) + 3(3 + 2 + 1) + 2(3 + 2 + 1) + 1(3 + 2 + 1)$

Each part has the common factor $(3 + 2 + 1)$ so we can write the entire expression like this:

$(3 + 2 + 1) (4 + 3 + 2 + 1)$

We've used the distributive property. Is the answer 60? (Yes.) We have the sum of the first 3 counting numbers times the sum of the first 4 counting numbers. Now we are looking for some way this relates to a 3 by 4 grid. Do you see a relationship? (Yes. The sum of the first 3 counting numbers times the sum of the first 4 counting numbers gives the number of different rectangles in a 3 by 4 grid.) Right! We found a new relationship. Now let's test it.

In the 3 by 2 grid we found 18 rectangles. Is $(3 + 2 + 1) (2 + 1) = 18$? (Yes.)

In the 2 by 2 grid we found 9 rectangles. Does $(2 + 1) (2 + 1) = 9$? (Yes.)

This means that *if* our rule is correct, the number of rectangles in a 5 by 5 grid is $(5 + 4 + 3 + 2 + 1) (5 + 4 + 3 + 2 + 1) = 225$.

Using the rule is a lot easier than counting!

Here is a final answer to our problem of finding the rule.
  To find the total number of rectangles in a c column by r row grid, multiply the sum of the first c counting numbers times the sum of the first r counting numbers. Using symbols we can write this as
  $(1 + 2 + \cdots + c) (1 + 2 + \cdots + r)$ or
  $$\frac{c(c + 1)}{2} \times \frac{r(r + 1)}{2}$$

That's an example of how some mathematical rules are discovered.

Caution: We never proved that our rule was right. That kind of proof comes later in your math studies.

1. BOUNCE, BOUNCE ...

Fay's rubber ball bounces exactly half the height from which it is dropped. She drops the ball from the top of a building that is 64 meters tall. How high will the ball bounce on its eighth bounce?

1. BOUNCE, BOUNCE . . .

Answer: 0.25 meter or 25 centimeters

About the Problem:

This warm-up for *Double Your Treasure* will give students some insights as to how rapidly a change occurs in numbers that are halved or doubled. This problem requires only simple division by two and some careful recording. Remember to have students estimate the answer *before* they begin.

Getting Started:

The problem is sufficiently easy so that most students won't require much help getting started. Here are some hints for those students who need them.

Draw a diagram of what is happening in the problem.

Carefully label your diagram.

Double check your figures.

Solution:

Students may make a chart, with or without a diagram. A common careless error will be to record the building height (64 meters) as the first bounce. The numbers in this problem are small and easy to work with so a calculator should not be needed.

Bounce	Height
1st	32 m
2nd	16 m
3rd	8 m
4th	4 m
5th	2 m
6th	1 m
7th	0.5 m
8th	0.25 m

Going Beyond:

1. How did your answer compare with your estimate?

2. If the ball had been dropped from twice the original height or 128 meters, how much difference would there be between the 8th bounces in each case? (0.5 m-0.25 m or 0.25 m)

3. If you are measuring to the *top* of the ball, will the bounce height ever reach zero? (No, because of the height of the ball.)

A goblin miner earns 1 cent the first day, 2 cents the second day, 4 cents the third day, 8 cents the fourth day, and so on, doubling the amount each day. How much will the miner earn in 30 days?

1. DOUBLE YOUR TREASURE

Answer: $10,737, 418.23 or $2^{30} - 1$

About the Problem:

Students should be asked to make an estimate of the solution on every non-routine problem they solve. They will be surprised by the answer to this problem if it is their first encounter with this type of problem.

This problem is usually not intimidating to students. It seems like a simple, but lengthy, addition problem. It is a good problem because it shows the power of mathematics and because the use of pattern simplifies the problem by reducing calculations.

If students have studied exponents, this is a good opportunity to see the daily earnings represented in exponential form: 2^0, 2^1, 2^2, 2^3, 2^4, . . ., 2^{29}.

Getting Started:

This problem requires many calculations. One mistake along the way will probably result in a wrong final answer. Students should be encouraged to make a neat, organized chart or table.

The problem is ideal for using the doubling feature on a calculator. Even with the help of the calculator, the 30 different amounts and totals need to be carefully checked.

These hints may be helpful to the student.

Make an estimate of the answer. Write it down. Check your estimate again after you've solved the problem.

Make a chart or table of the list of earnings each day. That is, list the amount you earn on the first day, the second, and so on.

Add to your chart a list of the total money earned by the end of each day.

Be on the lookout for patterns which may reveal shortcuts.

Solution:

Students are probably well advised to work out the parts of the solution one at a time. There will be many opportunities to make a careless addition error. The first two columns of the list would be written first. Then the total earnings would be computed and added to the chart.

Day of the Month	Daily Earnings	Total Earnings
1	1¢	1¢
2	2¢	3¢
3	4¢	7¢
4	8¢	15¢
5	16¢	31¢
6	32¢	63¢
.	.	.
.	.	.
.	.	.

Hopefully students will notice this pattern.

Daily Earnings		Total Earnings
1		
2	one less	1
4	one less	3
8	one less	7
16	one less	15
32	one less	31
64	one less	63

Observing this pattern will save many calculations. If students have studied exponents, they may recognize the Daily Earnings as powers of two. Combining the patterns and powers will give an answer of $2^{30} - 1$ or 1,073,741,823 cents. This amount is over ten million dollars. A partial table of the solution is given below.

Day of the Month	Daily Earnings	Total Earnings
1	1¢ (2^0)	1¢ (2^1-1)¢
2	2¢ (2^1)	3¢ (2^2-1)¢
3	4¢ (2^2)	7¢ (2^3-1)¢
4	8¢ (2^3)	15¢ (2^4-1)¢
5	16¢ (2^4)	31¢ (2^5-1)¢
6	32¢ (2^5)	63¢ (2^6-1)¢
.	.	.
.	.	.
.	.	.
28	134,217,728¢ (2^{27})	268,435,455¢ ($2^{28}-1$)¢
29	268,435,456¢ (2^{28})	536,870,911¢ ($2^{29}-1$)¢
30	536,870,912¢ (2^{29})	1,073,741,823¢ ($2^{30}-1$)¢

1. DOLLARS GROW

Your aunt will give you $1,000 if you invest it for 10 years in an account that pays 20% interest compounded annually. That is, at the end of each year your interest will be added to your account and invested at 20%.

What will your account be worth at the end of 10 years? How much interest will you earn during the tenth year?

1. DOLLARS GROW

Answer: $6,191.74

About the Problem:

This problem is nearly identical to *Double Your Treasure,* except that the multiplier is a decimal (1.2) instead of a whole number (2). Be sure students understand how compound interest works: the 20% interest is paid at the end of each year, and all interest is added to the savings and invested at 20%. That is, each year the interest becomes part of the principal.

Getting Started:

This is a good problem in which to use a calculator, but the computation is not too involved if a calculator is not available.

Hints to help the students get started might include

What is the interest for the first year?

What amount will be invested the second year?

Make a chart showing the interest and growing value of the savings.

Solution:

Most students will multiply the principle by 20% then add the interest to the principle. Hopefully, some insightful students will see that multiplying by 120% or 1.2 will accomplish the same thing. The chart below gives the year-by-year totals.

to start	$1000.00
interest (1st yr)	$200.00
end of year 1	$1200.00
interest (2nd yr)	$240.00
end of year 2	$1440.00
interest (3rd yr)	$288.00
end of year 3	$1728.00
interest (4th yr)	$345.60
end of year 4	$2073.60
interest (5th yr)	$414.72
end of year 5	$2488.32
interest (6th yr)	$497.66
end of year 6	$2985.98
interest (7th yr)	$597.20
end of year 7	$3583.18
interest (8th yr)	$716.64
end of year 8	4299.82
interest (9th yr)	$859.96
end of year 9	$5159.78
interest (10th yr)	1031.96
end of year 10	$6191.74

Thus, the total at the end of ten years is
$1,000 × 1.2 × 1.2 × 1.2 × 1.2 × 1.2 × 1.2 × 1.2 × 1.2 × 1.2 × 1.2
or $1,000 × $(1.2)^{10}$.

On most calculators the sequence of keystrokes to find the product is
1.2 × = = = = = = = = = × 1,000

Going Beyond:

1. How many years did it take for the investment to double? triple? (See solution.)

2. How could this problem be solved in a matter of seconds on a hand calculator? (See solution.)

3. Use a calculator to see what the $1000 would be worth if invested at 20% for 20 years. ($38,337.59) Will it be worth twice what it was worth in ten years? (No.)

4. This problem is an example of compound interest. Suppose the account paid 20% *simple* interest (principal x rate x time). How much would your account be worth at the end of 10 years? How much more would you earn in 10 years with compound interest?

2. CROSS SUM

In each cross puzzle below, place the numbers 1, 2, 3, 4, 5 in the squares, so that the sum of three numbers in a vertical or horizontal line equals the sum given above that puzzle.

sum = 8

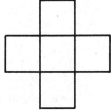

sum = 9

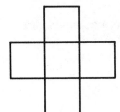

sum = 10

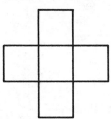

2. CROSS SUM

Answers:

Sum = 8

```
    2
  3 1 4
    5
```

Sum = 9

```
    1
  2 3 4
    5
```

Sum = 10

```
    1
  2 5 3
    4
```

About the Problem:

This is an easy three-part problem designed to give students confidence and practice with the guess-and-check strategy. You may need to clarify that a number can't be used twice. This problem will lead nicely into the *Sum of Thirteen* problem, if you discuss the process of listing all the combinations of a given sum.

Getting Started:

Let the students use trial and error here. In later more complex problems, they will see its limitations, and will begin to appreciate the advantages of using organized lists of combinations.

Some students might want to write the numbers 1 through 5 on separate slips of paper, and move them around within the puzzle until they find a correct solution.

Solution:

Most students will solve these puzzles by trial and error.

Going Beyond:

This is a good opportunity to discuss a way for the students to organize their trial-and-error approach. For example, consider the first part of the problem. We are looking for a sum of 8. What possible triples have a sum of 8?

$$1 - 2 - 5$$
$$1 - 3 - 4$$

There are only two possibilities. In the puzzle, one number must appear in both a column and a row. So 1 must be the number to place in the center of the puzzle. If 2 and 5 are placed in the column, then 3 and 4 must be placed in the row, and vice versa.

In a similar fashion, the students can list the number triples with sums of 9 and 10 to help solve the remaining two parts of the problem.

Remember that a rotation or a reflection of any puzzle solution is not considered a different solution.

Here is a good set of similar problems that are slightly more difficult.

Place the first six counting numbers in the circles below so that the sum on each side of the triangle is 9. Can you do this so that the sum is 10? 11? 12?

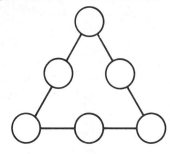

Have students make lists of combinations to help them solve the four puzzles.

Answers:

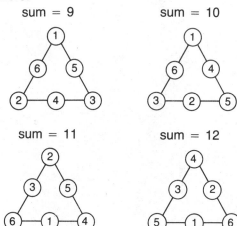

sum = 9   sum = 10

sum = 11   sum = 12

Place the numbers 1, 2, 3, 4, 5, 6, 7, 8 in the eight circles so that the sum of the numbers in any line equals 13.

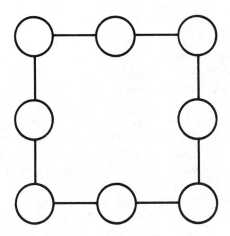

2. SUM OF THIRTEEN

Answer: Two possible solutions are

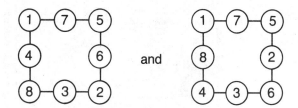

and

About the Problem:

This kind of problem gives students a chance to test their logic and organization ability as well as giving them some addition practice. The problem can be solved by trial and error but some good reasoning will shorten the solution process. The *Warm-up* problem which encourages students to list all combinations of a given sum helps prepare them for this problem.

Getting Started:

Observe the different ways students approach the problem. After the problem has been solved by several students, a discussion by the class on different ways to approach the problem may be particularly helpful to students the next time they encounter this type of problem.

Here are some hints.

Make a list of all of the three-number combinations of 1 through 8 that total 13.

Start with any number in one corner. Test its combinations on two sides of the square. Shift numbers and try different possibilities.

Solution:

A list of combinations provides a handy reference as the guess-and-check process begins.

sum = 13

1-8-4
1-7-5
2-8-3
2-7-4
2-6-5
3-6-4

Typical reasoning might be as follows:

"I will try 1 in a corner because it is in two combinations, 1-8-4 and 1-7-5. I will try 7 and 8 in corners that connect with 1. Eight uses 2 and 3 in its other combination. That's okay. I haven't used them yet. Seven uses 2 and 4 in its other combination. That won't work since I used 4 with 1-8-4. Therefore 7 can't be in the corner. I'll try 8 and 5 in the corners. That's okay because the other combination that uses 5 is 5-2-6. I haven't used 6 yet. Two must be used with 8 so it goes in a corner. All done. Check the sums. Are they all 13? Yes. I have a solution."

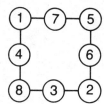

Going Beyond:

1. Now that you know how to solve this kind of problem, can you find a solution for a sum of 14?

Answer:

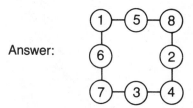

2. Can you solve this problem with a sum of 15?

Answer:

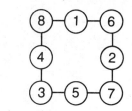

2. MAGIC SQUARE

Make a *magic square* by placing the digits 1 through 9 in the square below so that the sum of the three numbers in any vertical, horizontal, or diagonal line equals 15.

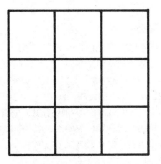

2. MAGIC SQUARE

Answer:

2	7	6
9	5	1
4	3	8

About the Problem:

It may be necessary to clarify that no number can be used twice. The sum of 15 must appear in three columns, three rows and two diagonals.

This is a classic problem. It was used as the extension problem because it is difficult without some practice on similar simpler problems. Depending on the ability of the students in your class, you may choose to give no initial hints. It may be advisable to let the students work on the problem over a period of two to four days. Warn students to show you the answer when they get it but not to tell other classmates.

Getting Started:

Students using only trial and error will soon see the complexity of the problem. After a period of experimenting with the problem, students may be ready for these helpful hints.

Make a list of all the combinations of the numbers 1 through 9 that total 15.

Which numbers are used most? Which are used least?

In the 3 by 3 square, which spaces are used in the most combinations? In the least combinations?

If students have not yet had much problem-solving success it may be best to give them one or two of the numbers of the solution. The problem will still require lots of good reasoning. Remember, success is vital in students' early problem-solving attempts. You, the teacher, know your students' needs and abilities better than anyone else.

Solution:

The following method of solution shows the value of an organized list. The combinations of the first nine counting numbers that total 15 are shown below.

```
      15
    9-1-5
    9-2-4
    8-1-6
    8-2-5
    8-3-4
    7-2-6
    7-3-5
    6-5-4
```

Notice we are looking for eight sums. Three vertical, three horizontal, and two diagonal.

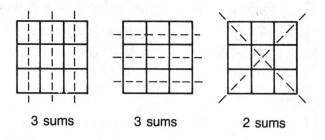

3 sums   3 sums   2 sums

If we can't find eight *different* combinations that total 15, we can't solve the problem. The organized listing above shows that we have found exactly eight. That's nice! A number in any corner will be used in three different sums. A number in the outside center position will be used in two sums. A number in the center will be used in four combinations.

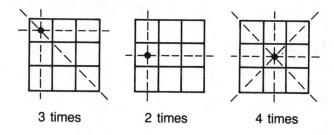

3 times   2 times   4 times

A summary of the number of times a number will be used in a sum of 15 is given below.

3	2	3
2	4	2
3	2	3

If we go back to the list of combinations that total 15, we could see how many times each number appears.

Numbers	Times used
1	2
2	3
3	2
4	3
5	4
6	3
7	2
8	3
9	2

(Continued on page 97)

3. SUM PATTERN

Find the following sum:

13 + 15 + 17 + 13 + 15 + 17 + 13 + 15 + 17 + 13 + 15 + 17 + 13 + 15 + 17 + 13 + 15 + 17

Look for patterns. (No calculators allowed.)

3. SUM PATTERN

Answer: 270

About the Problem:

This problem was specifically designed to have students look for easier ways to solve this problem than to consecutively add each of the 18 numbers. It should help prepare students to look for patterns in solving *Sum Fun* and its *Extension.*

Getting Started:

It may be necessary to tell students to look for patterns. It is best *not* to have a calculator to assist with this problem, because some students may use it to simply add all of the numbers, the very process we want them to avoid.

Solution:

There are many different approaches to this problem. We present three possible ones.

There are six sums of 13 + 15 + 17.
6 × (13 + 15 + 17) = 6 × 45 = 270

There are six 13s, six 15s, and six 17s all added together.
(6×13)+(6×15)+(6×17) = 78+90+102=270

The sum 13 + 17 is the same as the sum 15 + 15. So we have eighteen 15s to be added together.
18 × 15 = 270

Find a quick and easy method to compute the sum of the first 100 counting numbers. (No calculators allowed.)

$$1 + 2 + 3 + 4 + 5 + \cdots + 97 + 98 + 99 + 100$$

Answer: 5050

About the Problem:

This is a simple problem with no prerequisite skills needed other than being able to add whole numbers and discover a pattern.

A story is told about the famous mathematician, Carl Friedrich Gauss. When he was ten years old, his teacher presented the class with the perfect busy-work/drill problem, "Find the sum of the numbers 1 to 100." While his classmates scribbled industriously, Gauss sat thinking. Two minutes later, he had the correct answer. When he explained his method of solution, the problem seemed simple. His classmates doubtless moaned, "Why didn't I think of that?"

Mathematics is often described as the study of patterns. Unless we look for patterns and alternate solutions to problems, we won't find them. The story about Carl Friedrich Gauss may be an effective way to introduce this problem to the class. As George Polya once said, "A problem discovered is a problem rarely forgotten."

Getting Started:

Maybe writing the numbers horizontally will help students think of the "averaging" approach explained in the solution. Some students come up with problem-solving insights readily, others don't. Experience helps. The next time a student encounters a similar problem, he or she may try the technique used in the solution to this problem.

Here are some hints for students who have thought about the problem for several minutes but still have no ideas.

> What is the average number?

> What is the sum of the first and last numbers?

> What similar sums can you find?

On a problem such as this that requires an insight, it is better for the student to solve the problem with one or more hints than not to solve the problem at all. It is also important that some students have had an opportunity to discover the entire strategy themselves before any hints are given.

Solution:

Two slightly different approaches to the solution are shown below.

We see that the sum of the first and last numbers is 101.

$$1 + 2 + 3 + 4 \cdots + 97 + 98 + 99 + 100$$
$$\underbrace{\qquad\qquad}_{101}$$

As a matter of fact, we see that we can find many pairs whose sum is 101.

$$1 + 2 + 3 + 4 + \cdots + 97 + 98 + 99 + 100$$
(101, 101, 101)

How many 101s? 100? No, half that many. There are 50 pairs of numbers that each total 101. Our problem simplifies to 50×101 or 5050. Simple! Much easier than adding 100 numbers.

The second approach also requires a visual insight with the horizontal format. Reverse the sequence of the numbers and add it to the original sequence.

1	2	3	4	$\cdots$	97	98	99	100
100	99	98	97	$\cdots$	4	3	2	1
101	101	101	101	$\cdots$	101	101	101	101

This gives 100 sums of 101, or a total of 100×101. But we now have two sums of the first 100 counting numbers, so we divide this total by 2.

$$\frac{100 \times 101}{2} = 5050$$

Going Beyond:

1. Was it much faster to use the "short cut" method?

2. Isn't multiplication just a "short cut" method of addition?

3. Could you use this technique to find the sum of the first 1000 counting numbers? (Yes, the sum is 500,500.)

4. What happens if there is an odd number of numbers like $1 + 2 + 3 + 4 + \cdots + 23 + 24 + 25$? (It still works.) Can you discover a procedure for adding an odd number of consecutive counting numbers? (Still the sum of the first and last times the number of terms, divided by two.)

3. TRIANGULAR NUMBERS

A *triangular number* is a number that can be represented by dots arranged in a triangular shape as shown below. The first four triangular numbers are 1, 3, 6, 10. What is the 10th triangular number? The 20th? The 100th?

Triangular Numbers

1st	2nd	3rd	4th
•	••	•••	••••
1	3	6	10

3. TRIANGULAR NUMBERS

Answers: The 10th triangular number is 55.
The 20th triangular number is 210.
The 100th triangular number is 5050.

About the Problem:

Here is a good chance for students to apply what they learned in the problem *Sum Fun,* how to find the sum of a series of consecutive numbers.

Triangular numbers are part of the class of numbers called *figurate numbers.* Figurate numbers are numbers that can be displayed in specific geometric configurations. Other figurate numbers include square numbers, rectangular numbers, oblong numbers, pentagonal numbers, and hexagonal numbers. These numbers are interesting because of the patterns they contain. The triangular numbers are especially interesting because they appear frequently in other problems.

Getting Started:

Like the problem, *Sum Fun,* this problem is dependent upon either knowing or discovering how to find the sum of consecutive counting numbers. It also requires the insight to see the problem as the sum of consecutive counting numbers. If necessary, here are some hints.

Express the triangular number 10 as the sum of its rows.

Find a "short cut" way to add the rows of dots in the triangular number arrays.

Solution:

Using the Gauss method of adding consecutive numbers described in the solution to *Sum Fun,* we can make the table below.

Triangular number	Value	
1st	1	
2nd	3	(1+2)
3rd	6	(1+2+3)
4th	10	(1+2+3+4)
5th	15	(1+2+3+4+5)
•	•	
•	•	
•	•	
10th	55	(1+2+···+9+10)
•	•	
•	•	
•	•	
20th	210	(1+2+···+19+20)
•	•	
•	•	
•	•	
100th	5050	(1+2+···+99+100)

Going Beyond:

1. Can you devise a formula for finding the value of the nth triangular number? ($\frac{n(n+1)}{2}$; see the explanation below.)

$$1 + 2 + 3 + \cdots + (n - 2) + (n - 1) + n$$

There are $n/2$ pairs of numbers here, and each pair has a sum of $n + 1$. So the sum of all the pairs is $\frac{n}{2}(n + 1)$ or $\frac{n(n+1)}{2}$, which is the value of the nth triangular number.

2. Use a 4 by 4 dot array to illustrate that 16 is the sum of two consecutive triangular numbers.
   Answer:

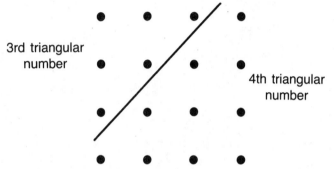

3rd triangular number

4th triangular number

3. Draw diagrams to illustrate that every square number is the sum of two triangular numbers. (Answers will vary.)

4. DIAGONAL COUNT

How many diagonals are in a hexagon?

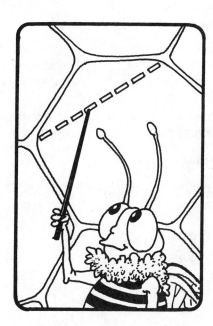

4. DIAGONAL COUNT

Answer: 9 diagonals

About the Problem:

This problem is quite easy and is a natural warm-up to *All Shook Up.* Hopefully, the obvious diagramming situation in this problem will suggest the same approach in the next problem.

It may be necessary to clarify that a diagonal is a line segment joining any two *nonadjacent* vertices.

Getting Started:

Suggest the students draw a diagram. Of course, any hexagon will do.

Solution:

The 9 diagonals are easily counted in a diagram.

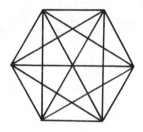

Going Beyond:

1. Were the diagonals easily counted?

2. If the problem had been a figure with 12 sides, would the diagonals be easily counted?

3. This problem has good extension possibilities but they should be delayed until *All Shook Up* and its *Extension* have been solved. The logical extension here is, "How many diagonals does a 24-sided polygon have? A 100-sided polygon? An *N*-sided polygon?"

Eight people meet at a party. They all exchange handshakes. How many handshakes are exchanged?

Answer: 28 handshakes

About the Problem:

No prerequisites are required here except counting. The problem is a good one because it can be approached in a variety of ways. It also provides an opportunity to be involved with combinations in which order is not important. That is, A shaking hands with B is the same handshake as B shaking hands with A. The obvious fact that no person shakes hands with himself may need to be pointed out to some students.

Getting Started:

This problem can be acted out by class members in front of the class. In order to record data, students may need to use names or symbols. See how they think this out on their own, then later discuss the advantages of using A, B, C, D, and so on.

Some helpful hints are

Can you draw a diagram that represents the problem?

Can you make a chart or list of all the handshakes?

Solution:

We represent the eight people by the letters A through H. Two styles of listing are shown below. The first is a tree diagram. The second is an organized listing of the pairs of people.

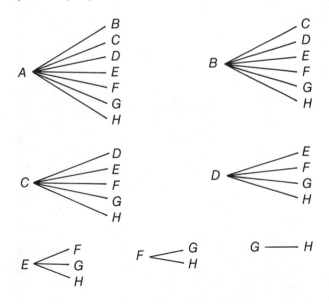

7 + 6 + 5 + 4 + 3 + 2 + 1 = 28 handshakes

Organized listing

AB,AC,AD,AE,AF,AG,AH
BC,BD,BE,BF,BG,BH
CD,CE,CF,CG,CH
DE,DF,DG,DH
EF,EG,EH
FG,FH
GH

Some students may prefer a geometric model. A line segment connecting points A and B could represent a handshake. The eight people could be modeled as shown in the figure below. Handshakes are counted as the problem solver connects A to B, A to C, A to D, and so on until each letter is connected to every other letter.

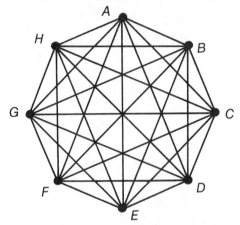

Some students will see the listing and diagramming as unnecessary. They may say, "Each of eight people shake hands with seven other people, so there are 7 times 8 or 56 handshakes." Some students that use this approach may overlook the fact that 7 times 8 counts A's shake with B and B's shake with A as two different elements. Other students will realize this and divide 56 by 2 to get the correct answer, 28.

Students should be encouraged to try whatever method they wish. They soon look for the easiest and fastest approach.

Going Beyond:

1. What were all the different methods used by class members to solve this problem?

2. After seeing these methods, which do you think is fastest?

3. If the problem had involved 100 people instead of eight, which method would be fastest? $\left(\dfrac{100 \times 99}{2} \right)$

4. JODY'S WARDROBE

Jody's favorite clothes include four T-shirts, three pairs of designer jeans, and two pairs of sandals. How many days in a row could she wear a different outfit using her favorite clothes?

4. JODY'S WARDROBE

Answer: 24 outfits

About the Problem:

It may be necessary to clarify that an outfit to be counted requires all three items, a T-shirt, a pair of jeans, and a pair of sandals. This problem gives students another opportunity to become familiar with tree diagrams and organized lists. In finding the total number of combinations, it doesn't matter which item of clothing comes first.

You may wish to discuss with the students some of the ways they could use symbols to represent the items as they make their tree diagram or organized list. A symbol should be simple and easy to remember. Natural symbols here would be T for T-shirt, J for jeans, and S for sandals. Since there are four T-shirts, we need some way to tell them apart. A common notation used by mathematicians is the subscript. The four T-shirts might be called T_1, T_2, T_3, and T_4. These symbols can be read, "the first T-shirt" or "T-shirt one," and so on. Similarly, the jeans could be called J_1, J_2, J_3, and the sandals S_1, S_2.

Getting Started:

Suggest that the students make tree diagrams (if they are familiar with that technique) or that they make a list. After they have worked on the problem, a discussion of different listing methods will be meaningful to them.

Solution:

A partial tree diagram is shown below.

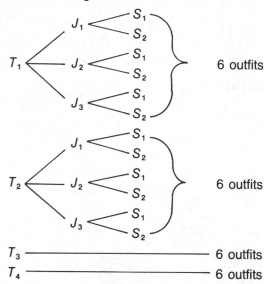

Thus, there are 24 different outfits for Jody to wear.

Making an organized listing of the different outfits is a bit more cumbersome, but certainly is a correct approach.

$$T_1J_1S_1, T_1J_2S_2, T_1J_3S_1, T_1J_1S_2, T_1J_2S_1, T_1J_3S_2$$
$$T_2J_1S_1, T_2J_2S_2, T_2J_3S_1, T_2J_1S_2, T_2J_2S_1, T_2J_3S_2$$
$$T_3J_1S_1, T_3J_2S_2, T_3J_3S_1, T_3J_1S_2, T_3J_2S_1, T_3J_3S_2$$
$$T_4J_1S_1, T_4J_2S_2, T_4J_3S_1, T_4J_1S_2, T_4J_2S_1, T_4J_3S_2$$

Again, we find 24 different outfits.

Going Beyond:

Have the students create tree diagrams for this problem using a different order for the three items, such as sandals—jeans—T-shirts.

Hopefully, some students will observe that the answer is simply the product of the number of items, $4 \times 3 \times 2 = 24$. This "rule" for calculating the answer justifies some exploration. Have students make up some other examples of simple tree diagrams to test the idea of a general rule about this type of combination problem. They will discover that this method, the multiplication principle of combinations, does work in all cases.

5. RED AND WHITE CUBE

A 3 by 3 by 3 cube can be built with red cubes and white cubes so that no white faces touch and no red faces touch. How would you do this? How many small red faces and how many small white faces will be visible on the large cube?

5. RED AND WHITE CUBE

Answer: Use 14 red cubes and 13 white. Then 25 red faces and 20 white faces will be visible. (Note: the colors red and white can be interchanged in the solution.)

About the Problem:

This warm-up for the *Red Paint* problem will require students to deal with the third dimension. Students having little or no problem-solving experience should actually build the model out of blocks. If blocks are not used, students will need to struggle with diagrams to represent the problem.

Getting Started:

Build the cube with blocks.

Draw pictures of the block.

How many faces show on each side?

How many faces can be seen altogether?

Solution:

The cube is a checkerboard cube. It contains 14 of one color and 13 of the other. When the cube is assembled, 25 faces of one color and 20 of the other color will be visible.

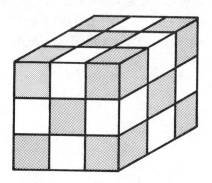

Going Beyond:

1. Will edges of the same color touch? (No)
2. How many blocks can't be seen at all? (2)

There are 27 small cubes arranged in a 3 by 3 by 3 cube. The top and sides of the large cube are painted red. How many of the 27 small cubes have 0 faces painted? 1 face? 2 faces? 3 faces? 4 faces? 5 faces? 6 faces?

5. RED PAINT

Answers: 2 cubes have 0 faces painted.
9 cubes have 1 face painted.
12 cubes have 2 faces painted.
4 cubes have 3 faces painted.
No cube has more than 4 faces painted.

About the Problem:

This problem offers students an opportunity to test their spacial perception. It requires some systematic organization of counting and recording. It is not a difficult problem for most students. However, it seems to invite careless errors. It is interesting to watch the different ways that students go about organizing their data and analyzing the problem. This problem lends itself to discussion of different ways to organize after the class has solved it.

Getting Started:

Modeling is the key here. Will the students choose to approach it two-dimensionally, three-dimensionally or actually try to record information from their mental image of the figure?

Draw diagrams that help.

Make a model with wooden blocks.

Check to be sure you've accounted for all 27 cubes.

Solution:

Shown below are three layer diagrams which account for all 27 blocks. Drawings of the sides may be more confusing since they will not include all blocks. Also, side drawings introduce possible double counting of the corners.

Number of Painted Faces

3	2	3
2	1	2
3	2	3

2	1	2
1	0	1
2	1	2

2	1	2
1	0	1
2	1	2

top layer   middle layer   bottom layer

A frequency distribution from the layer diagrams reveals the solution.

Number of faces painted	Number of cubes
0	2
1	9
2	12
3	4
4	0
5	0
6	0

Going Beyond:

A rectangular prism was made of cubes. The cubes were arranged 3 high, 5 wide, and 6 long. The top and sides were painted. How many cubes were painted on 0 faces? (24) On 1 face? (40) On 2 faces? (22) On 3 faces? (4)

5. MULTICOLORED CUBE

Arrange 9 red cubes, 9 blue cubes, and 9 white cubes in a large 3 by 3 by 3 cube so that no row or column of cubes contains two cubes of the same color.

5. MULTICOLORED CUBE

Answer: Answers will vary. See the sample answer in the Solution section below.

About the Problem:

This may be more of a problem in diagramming a three-dimensional figure than solving the actual problem. If students have already worked on *Red Paint,* then diagramming the three layers of the cube may be an obvious approach.

Young students or those who still lack confidence in their problem-solving skills may benefit most from this problem by actually building the model with blocks.

Clarify that three blocks in a diagonal line may have the same colors, but not three blocks in a row or column.

Getting Started:

Build a model with blocks (teacher's option).

Draw a diagram of the problem to help you.

Solution:

There are numerous correct solutions. Solutions are most easily seen in three layers.

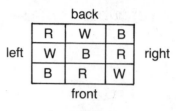

bottom layer

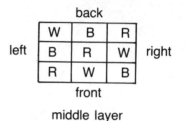

middle layer

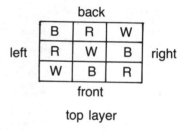

top layer

Going Beyond:

1. Did you think of representing the blocks in layers?

2. Is there an easier way?

3. Place any of the numbers 1 through 5 in a 3 by 3 square so that no three numbers in a horizontal, vertical, or diagonal line are alike.
   One possible answer:

4	1	2
3	5	4
1	2	3

6. ONE-TWO-THREE

How many different two-digit numbers and how many different three-digit numbers can be written using the digits 1, 2, and 3? (Use each digit only once in a number.)

6. ONE-TWO-THREE

Answers: 6 two-digit numbers
6 three-digit numbers

About the Problem:

This problem is very similar to *Digit Alice,* but easier. Students will see a need for a systematic way to list the numbers.

Solution:

One way to count the two-digit and three-digit numbers is to use tree diagrams, as shown below.

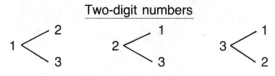

Another way to solve this problem is to make organized lists of the different numbers.

Two-digit numbers

  12, 13
  21, 23
  31, 32

Three-digit numbers

  123, 132
  213, 231
  312, 321

By either method, we can count the 6 two-digit and 6 three-digit numbers.

How many different three-digit numbers can be written using the digits 4, 5, 6, and 7? (Use each digit only once in a number.)

3-DIGIT NUMBERS

Answer: 24 three-digit numbers

About the Problem:

This problem differs from previous combination problems in that the order of the elements is important. The number 456 is a different number than 654. A tree diagram or organized list will lead to the solution. There is an opportunity here for bright beginning problem solvers to discover a new kind of application of a multiplication principle.

If you wish to introduce the concepts of *combinations* and *permutations,* this is a good problem for that purpose. Recall that a *combination* is an arrangement in which order *is not* important. A *permutation* is an arrangement in which order *is* important. For example, there is one combination of the letters A, B and C. There are six permutations of the letters A, B and C. Namely ABC, ACB, BAC, BCA, CAB and CBA. The *Extension* problem will give students more practice with this concept.

Getting Started:

Draw a tree diagram or make an organized list.

Check your list to make sure it is complete.

Solution:

The tree diagram is shown below. Often, after students complete the first diagram they think, "Oh, there are 6 numbers that start with 4, so there will be 6 numbers that start with 5, 6 and 7. Four times 6 is 24." Since the problem asked for the number of numbers and not a list of all the different numbers, the above reasoning should be accepted and encouraged.

There are 24 different three-digit numbers.

Going Beyond:

A simple way to compute permutations is to use the following multiplication principle. You are writing a three-digit number using the digits 4, 5, 6 and 7 with no repeats. You start by writing the hundreds digit. There are 4 choices.

4 choices here (4, 5, 6 or 7)

Once you've written a digit, say 7, in the hundreds place, there are 3 choices left for the tens place.

3 choices here (4, 5 or 6)

Once you've written a digit in the tens place, say 4, there are 2 choices left for the ones place.

2 choices here (5 or 6)

So there are 4 choices × 3 choices × 2 choices which gives 24 permutations.

$$\boxed{4} \times \boxed{3} \times \boxed{2} = 24$$

Have the students test this method on the following problem:

How many two-digit numbers can be written using the digits 1, 3, 5, 7 and 9 (no repeats)?

Short method:

5 choices here then 4 choices here

$$\boxed{5} \times \boxed{4} = 20$$

Were there 20? Make a tree diagram to check this answer.

Here's another problem in which students can use the multiplication principle.

How many four-digit numbers can be made using odd digits with no digit repeated?

$$(\boxed{5} \times \boxed{4} \times \boxed{3} \times \boxed{2} = 120)$$

6. WIN, PLACE, AND SHOW

Eight runners are entered in the 1000-meter run. How many different first, second, and third place finishes could possibly occur?

6. WIN, PLACE, AND SHOW

Answer: 336 finishes

About the Problem:

This is a difficult problem for beginners unless they have successfully solved similar problems like *4. Extension* and *Digit Alice.*

If the wording of the problem seems ambiguous to some, here is further clarification. If runners are designated *A, B, C, D, E, F, G* and *H,* then finishes would include *ABC, ACB, DEF, FED,* and so on. Making a complete list here is out of the question since there are more than three hundred *permutations.* (See the *Digit Alice* discussion.) Students will need to apply or discover the multiplication principle to easily solve this problem.

Getting Started:

Start a tree diagram or organized list.

Look for a pattern.

Find a short cut solution without listing and counting all the possible finishes.

Solution:

The simple way to solve this problem is to use the previously explained multiplication principle. Any of the 8 runners could place first. Once first place is established, any of the other 7 runners could place second. Finally, any of the other 6 runners could place third. The solution is simply $8 \times 7 \times 6$ or 336.

If students begin a tree diagram or listing, they may reason that 42 different finishes could occur if A won, so each of the 8 runners would have 42 possible different finishes. Thus, the answer must be 8×42 or 336.

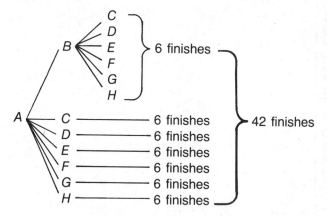

Going Beyond:

1. If $8 \times 7 \times 6$ gives the answer for the possible first three finishes, what do you suppose would give the answer for the possible first two finishes? (8×7) First four finishes? ($8 \times 7 \times 6 \times 5$)

2. Use a calculator to figure every possible way all eight runners could finish. ($8 \times 7 \times 6 \times 5 \times 4 \times 3 \times 2 \times 1$ or 40,320) Note: This is a good place to introduce students to the meaning of *factorial.* 8! is read eight factorial. $8! = 8 \times 7 \times 6 \times 5 \times 4 \times 3 \times 2 \times 1$.

7. FIRST FOUR

Using all four of the numbers 1, 2, 3, 4 and the operations $+, -, \times, \div$, make equations that equal 0 through 10. (You may use the numbers and operations in any order, and you may use an operation more than once.)

Example: $(2 \times 3) - 4 + 1 = 3$

7. FIRST FOUR

Answer: Answers will vary. See the sample answers in the Solution section below.

About the Problem:

Parentheses may be needed in some cases to clarify the order of operations. (See the *Equation Puzzle* discussion.) Although this is basically a trial-and-error problem, students will probably do much mental arithmetic in solving it. The advantage of a problem that has multiple parts or solutions such as this is that once a student gets started and develops some confidence, he or she has an opportunity to practice and develop the skill or strategy involved.

Getting Started:

Try experimenting first with just addition and subtraction.

You may need to use parentheses, as in the example, to clarify your answer.

Solution:

There may be several different solutions that give the same number.

Sample answers:

$(4 + 1) - (2 + 3) = 0$
$(3 \times 2) - 4 - 1 = 1$
$4 - 3 + 2 - 1 = 2$
$(2 \times 3) - 4 + 1 = 3$
$4 + 3 - 2 - 1 = 4$
$1 \times (4 \div 2) + 3 = 5$
$4 + 3 - 2 + 1 = 6$
$(4 + 3) \times (2 - 1) = 7$
$(4 + 3) + (2 - 1) = 8$
$1 \times (4 + 3 + 2) = 9$
$1 + 2 + 3 + 4 = 10$

Going Beyond:

1. How do parentheses help clarify a solution? (They determine the order of operations.)

2. Which numbers can be written with different solutions? (All of them.)

3. For which of the numbers 11 through 20 can equations be created? (All of them. See the equations below.)

$(4 \times 2) + (3 \times 1) = 11$
$(4 \times 2) + 3 + 1 = 12$
$(4 \times 3) + 2 - 1 = 13$
$(4 \times 3) + (2 \times 1) = 14$
$(4 \times 3) + (2 + 1) = 15$
$4 \times (3 + 2 - 1) = 16$
$3 \times (4 + 2) - 1 = 17$
$3 \times (4 + 2 \times 1) = 18$
$3 \times (4 + 2) + 1 = 19$
$(4 \times 1) \times (3 + 2) = 20$

Using all four of the numbers 8, 4, 2, 1 *in that order,* make equations that equal 0 through 10. (You may use the operations $+$, $-$, $\times$, $\div$ in any order and any number of times.)

Example: $8 - 4 + (2 \times 1) = 6$

7. EQUATION PUZZLE

Answer: Answers will vary. See the sample answers in the Solution section below.

About the Problem:

This problem is like its *Warm-up* except for the fact that the four numbers must appear in each equation in the order 8, 4, 2 and 1.

It will be essential to explain to students either before or after this problem, the use of parentheses and the order of operations. The reason this is critical here is that an expression like $8 - 4 \times 2 \times 1$ would have the value of 8 if the operations were done from left to right, or the value 0 if all multiplications were done first. Mathematicians have agreed upon the following rules:

1. Do all multiplications and divisions first from left to right.
2. Then do all additions and subtractions from left to right.

This means that without any parentheses to indicate which part or parts of the equation are to be treated as separate numbers, the value of the expression above is 0. If the value is meant to be 8, then parentheses must be inserted, $(8 - 4) \times 2 \times 1 = 8$.

If may be good to set up a few problems without parentheses and evaluate them for practice. Then have students insert parentheses to give a different value.

Example: $4 + 3 \times 2 - 1 = 9$
$(4 + 3) \times (2 - 1) = 7$

Getting Started:

Remember to keep the numbers in the proper order.

Try experimenting with different combinations of addition and subtraction.

Record each different answer.

Solution:

Students often see that while attempting to create an equation for one specific number they come up with a solution for a different number. A good strategy, then, in this kind of problem is to experiment initially not looking for specific answers. When several answers have been discovered, it becomes time for the problem solver to begin looking for the equations giving specific numbers that haven't yet been found.

Sample answers:

$8 - (4 \times 2) \times 1 = 0$
$8 - 4 - 2 - 1 = 1$
$8 - 4 - (2 \times 1) = 2$
$8 - 4 - 2 + 1 = 3$
$(8 \div 4) + (2 \times 1) = 4$
$8 - 4 + 2 - 1 = 5$
$8 - 4 + 2 \times 1 = 6$
$8 - 4 + 2 + 1 = 7$
$8 \times [(4 \div 2) - 1] = 8$
$8 + 4 - 2 - 1 = 9$
$8 + (4 \div 2) \times 1 = 10$

Going Beyond:

1. Which answers have more than one solution?

2. Is it possible to form equations that equal 11 through 20?

   Sample answers:

   $(8 + 4) - (2 - 1) = 11$
   $(8 + 4) \times (2 - 1) = 12$
   $(8 + 4) + (2 - 1) = 13$
   $(8 + 4) + (2 \times 1) = 14$
   $8 + 4 + 2 + 1 = 15$
   $8 + [(4 \times 2) \times 1] = 16$
   $8 + [(4 \times 2) + 1] = 17$
   $8 + [4 \times (2 + 1)] = 20$

7. FOUR FOURS

Using exactly four 4s and the operations
+, −, x, and ÷, make equations that equal
0, 1, 2, 3, 4, 5, 6, 7, 8, and 9.

7. FOUR FOURS

Answer: Answers will vary. See the sample answers in the Solution section below.

About the Problem:

This problem is slightly different from *Equation Puzzle,* and its *Warm-up.* If students seem to like this kind of problem and/or if some students are finally "catching on," it will be worthwhile to follow up with a similar problem. Often a two-week break from a particular type of problem will test students' understanding.

Getting Started:

Students will have no difficulty getting started if they have worked *Equation Puzzle* and its *Warm-up.*

Solution:

There may be several different solutions that give the same number.

Sample answers:

$$4 + 4 - 4 - 4 = 0$$
$$(4 \div 4) + (4 - 4) = 1$$
$$(4 \div 4) + (4 \div 4) = 2$$
$$(4 + 4 + 4) \div 4 = 3$$
$$(4 - 4) \times 4 + 4 = 4$$
$$(4 \times 4 + 4) \div 4 = 5$$
$$[(4 + 4) \div 4] + 4 = 6$$
$$4 + 4 - (4 \div 4) = 7$$
$$(4 \times 4 \div 4) + 4 = 8$$
$$4 + (4 \div 4) + 4 = 9$$

Going Beyond:

A much tougher classic problem is to make an equation that equals each of the first 100 counting numbers, using four 4s. In this problem any math operations can be used, such as $\sqrt{\ }$, !, exponents, and so on.

8. FRAME GAME

How many different rectangles can you count in this figure?

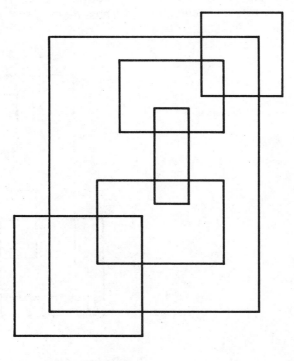

8. FRAME GAME

Answer: 15 rectangles

About the Problem:

Both this and the *Star Stitch* problem provide some practice and build confidence for the *Extension* problem. The solution of the *Extension* uses more different strategies than any other problem in this book. It is a super problem!

Getting Started:

First count the single rectangles.

Next count the combined.

Double check to make sure you've counted them all.

Be careful. Thorough counting pays off in this problem.

Solution:

Dividing the problem into numbered regions as shown below gives some reference points. Twelve of the rectangles have been numbered. In addition, there are three more rectangles: 5 and 6; 6 and 7; and 5, 6 and 7. Thus, there are 15 rectangles in the figure.

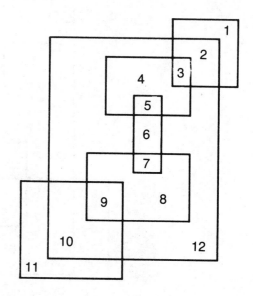

Going Beyond:

1. Is a square a rectangle? (Yes.)

2. Make a similar rectangle puzzle yourself. Solve your puzzle. Exchange puzzles with a fellow student. Do your answers agree?

How many different triangles are in this star?

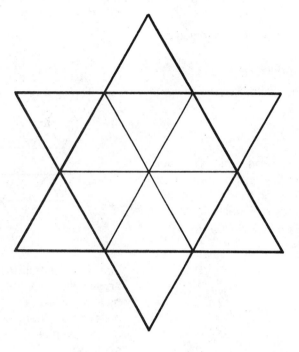

8. STAR STITCH

Answer: 20 triangles

About the Problem:

Like its *Warm-up,* this is a simple counting problem. The classic problem here is the *Extension* to this problem. *Star Stitch* should serve to give the students a little confidence and a systematic approach.

Getting Started:

Start by counting single triangles, that is, triangles with one unit on a side.

Next count triangles with two units on a side.

Some triangles point up, some down. Be sure to count them all.

Solution:

First, count all the triangles with one unit on a side. There are 6 pointing up and 6 pointing down. Next, count the triangles with two units on a side. There are 3 pointing up and 3 pointing down. Finally, there is 1 triangle with three units on a side pointing up, and 1 pointing down. Thus there are 6 + 6 + 3 + 3 + 1 + 1 = 20 triangles in the star.

Going Beyond:

The 20 triangles in the star were not too difficult to count. The more complex the figure, the more important it is to have a systematic approach to find the solution. For example, if each small triangle in the star figure were divided into four smaller triangles by connecting the three midpoints, the figure would be much more complex. Could you find the total number of different triangles in this figure? Guess first.

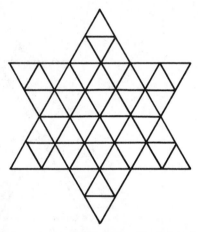

First count small triangles (point up). Then count triangles with two units on a side and so on. When you have counted all of the point-up triangles, do you believe that there will be the same number of point-down triangles? (Yes.) Why? (Because the figure is symmetrical.)

Units on a side	Number of triangles pointing up
1	24
2	15
3	10
4	6
5	3
6	1

59 Total

Pointing up   59
Pointing down   59
Total   118

Notice that there are some triangular numbers in this chart: 1, 3, 6, 10, 15. They were discussed in problem *3. Extension.*

8. FIND THE RULE

Discover the rule for finding the number of different rectangles in a square grid containing *c* columns and *r* rows.

8. FIND THE RULE

Answer: The number of rectangles in a *c* column by *r* row grid is the sum of the first *c* counting numbers times the sum of the first *r* counting numbers.

Solution:

See pages ix -xiv.

About the Problem:

Caution. This is a difficult problem but an excellent one. It is the author's favorite because it requires many different problem-solving techniques. This problem may offer the most mileage to beginning problem solvers if presented as a problem for the entire class to solve. You should present questions, clarify situations and lead the class through the problem using the discovery teaching technique. A sample development, written as a teacher might present the problem for class solution, is presented on pages ix - xiv. The problem presented this way will take one to two class periods.

Although the problem is a challenging one, it requires no mathematical prerequisites other than counting, factoring and use of the distributive property.

9. FOUR SQUARES

Find the five different shapes that can be made using four squares which share at least one edge with another square.

Note: These squares share an edge.

These squares do not share an edge.

9. FOUR SQUARES

Answer:

About the Problem:

This is a simpler version of *Paintominoes.* You may need to clarify which configurations are acceptable. Squares must share a complete edge as shown below.

right   wrong

A shape that has been rotated or reflected to another position is not considered a different shape. As soon as students have solved this problem, you may wish to give them the *Paintominoes* problem.

Getting Started:

Use cubes or square tiles to explore this problem. (Don't stack the squares.)

Or explore it on graph paper.

Or draw your own squares.

Solution:

Students will find the five shapes through trial and error.

Going Beyond:

1. How did you think about exploring the possibilities?

2. How did you organize your exploration so that you'd be sure to find all the shapes?

There are 12 different shapes that can be made using five squares with common edges. The shapes are called *pentominoes.*

    Example:

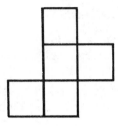

Can you find all 12 pentominoes?

9. PAINTOMINOES

Answer:

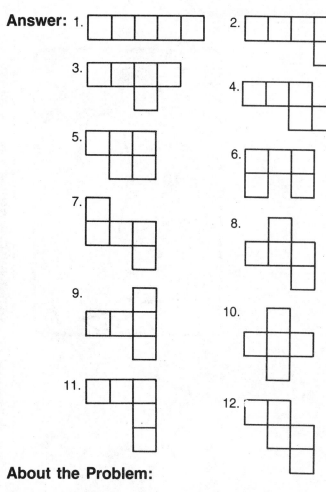

Each square must share at least one edge with another square.

right

wrong

Getting Started:

Most students shouldn't have trouble getting started once it has been clarified what "different shapes" means.

Make models of the shapes using cubes, square tiles, or graph paper. Remember, squares cannot be stacked.

What different shapes could be made using four squares?

What five-square shapes could be created from each of the four-square shapes?

Solution:

Although students will use trial and error to solve this problem, it will be necessary for them to organize their work. Otherwise, they will either miss some shapes or include some duplicates. The sequence of shapes shown in the answer above illustrates one possible organization scheme.

About the Problem:

This problem involves the use of visual perception and organizational skills. There are a couple of ambiguities that may need to be clarified before starting the problem. A shape is *not* considered to be different if it is rotated to a different position.

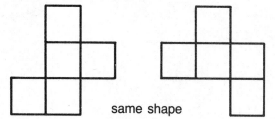

same shape

Also, a shape is not considered to be different if it is a reflection of a shape.

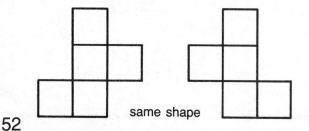

same shape

Going Beyond:

1. Draw the 12 shapes on the chalkboard and number them.
   a. Which shapes would fit onto themselves if rotated 180° or a half turn? (#1, #7, and #10)
   b. Which shapes would fit onto themselves if rotated a quarter turn or 90°? (#10)
   c. Which shapes would fit onto themselves if flipped or reflected? (#1, #6, #9, and #10)
   The shapes that fit onto themselves, if rotated, have rotational symmetry. The shapes that fit onto themselves if reflected have line symmetry, mirror symmetry, or reflective symmetry.

2. If you were to work the same problem using six squares, what would be the best way to assure that you found all possibilities? (One way is to move one square around in each possible position on each of the 12 solutions with five squares.)

(Continued on page 98)

9. POLYGON PARADE

Show how four identical isosceles right triangles can be placed together to form
  A. a rectangle that isn't a square.
  B. two different parallelograms that aren't rectangles
  C. a square
  D. a triangle
  E. a trapezoid

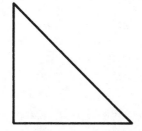

Isosceles right triangle

9. POLYGON PARADE

Answer: A. Rectangle that isn't a square

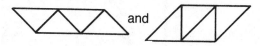

B. Two different parallelograms that aren't rectangles

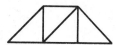

C. A square

D. A triangle

E. A trapezoid

Getting Started:

It is often interesting to observe the different ways that students approach problems. This problem is a visual one. Some students will be satisfied to sketch diagrams. Others will seek out or create triangular pieces to manipulate. Although this problem is easy enough for most students to solve without physical models, if the problem were any more challenging, physical models would definitely help find the solution. If some students have difficulty drawing all the possibilities, suggest that they cut the four pieces out of paper or cardboard.

Solution:

Students will solve this problem by trial and error.

About the Problem:

This problem involves mentally or physically manipulating geometric shapes to create combined shapes. Elementary students may need to know that an isosceles right triangle contains two equal (congruent) sides and one right angle. A trapezoid is a four-sided figure with two sides parallel and two non-parallel. A parallelogram is a four-sided figure with both pairs of opposite sides parallel. It is assumed in this problem that the triangles will be placed with equal sides touching. No overlapping is allowed.

10. DRAW ONE

What are the chances of drawing a red card from a regular 52-card deck of playing cards? What are the chances of drawing a spade? A 5? A black 3? A 7 of clubs?

10. DRAW ONE

Answers: Red Card: 1/2
Spade: 1/4
5: 1/13
Black 3: 1/26
7 of clubs: 1/52

About the Problem:

A good deal of the mathematics we use in our daily lives involves chance. Although students are often not given formal definitions of probabilities, they are usually familiar with ways to express chance from weather reports, sporting events, elections, and other events.

It is assumed that all students are familiar with a standard 52-card deck of playing cards.

Getting Started:

If students are *not* familiar with standard playing cards, the following questions may help.

How many suits are in a deck of cards?

What are the suit names?

What cards are in each suit?

How do we express chances? (_____ out of _____, as a fraction, a ratio or a percent)

Solution:

A. There are 13 hearts, 13 diamonds and 52 cards altogether, so the chances of drawing a card of a red suit are 26 out of 52 or 26/52 or 1/2.

B. There are 13 spades, so the chances of drawing a spade are 13 out of 52 or 13/52 or 1/4.

C. There are four 5s, one in each suit, so the chances of drawing a 5 are 4 out of 52 or 4/52 or 1/13.

D. The only two black 3s are the 3 of clubs and the 3 of spades, so the chances of drawing a black 3 are 2 out of 52 or 2/52 or 1/26.

E. Since there is only one 7 of clubs, the chance of drawing it is 1 out of 52 or 1/52.

Going Beyond:

1. The chances of an event occurring are often referred to as a probability. What is the probability of drawing a face card, that is, a King, Queen, or Jack? (3/13)

2. What is the probability of drawing a card less than 6? Assume that Ace is high. (4/13)

3. If you are trying to draw an Ace from a full deck, and you don't succeed on the first draw, what are the chances on the second draw if you don't replace the first card you drew? (4/51)

The triangle shown below is called *Pascal's triangle.* What numbers are in the next row of this triangle? What patterns can you find in the rows and diagonals of the triangle?

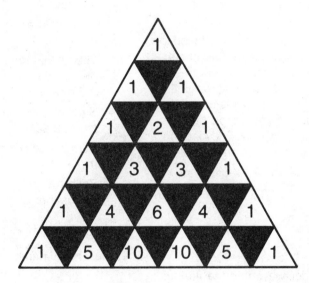

Answers: The next row is 1, 6, 15, 20, 15, 6, 1. See the patterns listed in the solution below.

About the Problem:

The Pascal Triangle number pattern is named after the French mathematician and philosopher Blaise Pascal. Pascal lived during the period 1623 to 1662. He was very interested in the mathematics involved with chance events.

Even though students may not have been introduced to elementary probability concepts yet, the patterns generated by the triangular array present a puzzle by themselves. When referring to rows, the first row is the one with only two ones in it. The top row is called the zero row. This makes it easy to reference the row number by the second number in the row. The diagonal columns of the triangle are referenced as shown below.

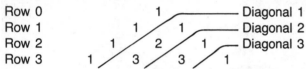

Row 0   1 —————— Diagonal 1
Row 1   1   1 ———— Diagonal 2
Row 2   1   2   1 —— Diagonal 3
Row 3   1   3   3   1

Getting Started:

Study the triangle and look for ways that the various numbers could have been generated (created).

How does each number relate to the number near it in a row or column?

Solution:

A number is always the sum of the two numbers diagonally above it. The 6th row would be

$$1 \quad 5 \quad 10 \quad 10 \quad 5 \quad 1$$
$$1 \quad 6 \quad 15 \quad 20 \quad 15 \quad 6 \quad 1$$

Here are the most common patterns. Students may discover others.

1. All ones in the first diagonal.
2. Consecutive counting numbers in the second diagonal.
3. Triangular numbers in the third diagonal. (See the discussion of triangular numbers in problem 3. *Extension.*)
4. Sum of consecutive triangular numbers in the fourth diagonal.
5. Sum of each row is twice the sum of the previous row.
6. Each row is symmetrical; that is, it is the same from either direction.

Going Beyond:

1. How many numbers are in the 10th row of Pascal's Triangle? (11) In the 100th? (101) In the nth row? ($n + 1$)

2. Find the sum of the first few rows. Do you see a pattern? What is it? (power of two) What is the sum of the numbers in the 10th row? (2^{10}) the 100th? (2^{100})

10. WIN A TRIP?

Three students will represent your school at a conference at the state capitol. A drawing will be held to select the three representatives from a group of five finalists. If you and your friend are both finalists, what are the chances that both of your names will be drawn?

10. WIN A TRIP?

Answer: 3/10

About the Problem:

This problem relates to *Pascal's Triangle*. Students need to understand that their chances are represented by the number of different ways their name could be drawn compared to the total number of ways all names could be drawn.

If you feel your students may not be ready for this problem, it could be worked as a class problem by making lists and soliciting from the class as much information about the problem and its solution as possible.

Getting Started:

Make a list of all combinations of names that could be drawn.

How many of these include your winning a trip?

How many of these include both you and your friend?

Solution:

Let the five students involved in the final selection be represented by letters. Suppose *A* represents the student figuring his chances, and *B* represents the friend. The combinations could be any of the following: *ABC, ABD, ABE, ACD, ACE, ADE, BCD, BCE, BDE* and *CDE.*

Since *A* and *B* appear in 3 of the 10 possible combinations, the chances of you and your friend being selected together are 3/10.

Going Beyond:

1. Did *A* and *B* have a better than 50-50 chance of both being selected? (No.)

2. Did all finalists have the same chance? (Yes.)

3. After the first name was drawn, and it wasn't *A*'s name, what were *A*'s chances? (2/4)

4. This problem offers an opportunity to look back and relate the combinations to Pascal's triangle. We have found the number of ways (10) in which three names can be drawn from a set of five names. Look at the fifth row of Pascal's triangle. Its entries represent different combinations of five objects.

1	5	10	10	5	1
5 objects taken 0 at a time	5 objects taken 1 at a time	5 objects taken 2 at a time	5 objects taken 3 at a time	5 objects taken 4 at a time	5 objects taken 5 at a time
none of people	A, B, C, D, E,	AB, AC, AD, AE, BC, BD, BE, CD, CE, DE	ABC, ABD, ABE, ACD, ACE, ADE, BCD, BCE, BDE, CDE	ABCD, ABCE, ABDE, ACDE, BCDE	ABCDE

11. PRIME SEARCH

The sum of the digits of an odd two-digit prime number is 11. The tens digit is greater than the ones digit. What is the number?

11. PRIME SEARCH

Answer: 83

About the Problem:

This type of deductive logic problem is good for beginning problem solvers. Students may be able to create good problems of their own with a little practice. Those students who are unfamiliar with primes should do problem *15. Warm-up* before solving this problem.

Getting Started:

Students shouldn't have trouble getting started with this problem. The approach is a simple process of elimination.

Which combinations of two digits total 11?

Which of these are odd?

Which are prime?

Which of these numbers have their tens digit greater than the units digit?

Solution:

We start with one piece of information. Then we test the other information against the starting information. We eliminate inappropriate numbers as we check out each piece of information. The information given in the problem could be written as statements.

It is a two-digit number.

It is an odd number.

It is a prime number.

The sum of the digits is 11.

The tens digit is greater than the units digit.

Let's start by listing the two-digit numbers which have a digit-sum of 11.

29, 38, 47, 56, 65, 74, 83, 92

Since the number we want is odd, we can eliminate the even numbers, leaving

29, 47, 65, 83

We want the number to be prime, so we eliminate the composite numbers, leaving

29, 83, 47

Finally, only 83 has its tens digit greater than its units digit. So the answer must be 83.

Going Beyond:

If the word "composite" was substituted for "prime" in the problem, what would be the answer? (65)

A woman wants to take her fox, chicken, and bag of corn across the river in her canoe. The canoe can hold only one thing in addition to the woman. If left alone, the fox would eat the chicken, or the chicken would eat the corn. How can the woman take everything across the river safely?

11. CANOE SOLVE THIS?

Answer: See the Solution section.

About the Problem:

This classic problem involves logic and some diagramming. It is a good idea to read the problem through more than once. The problem, already long and wordy, assumes that the fox doesn't like corn.

Students should not "think out loud" or attempt to explain the problem before others have had a chance to quietly work through the problem themselves. Often a person solves a problem correctly, but gets confused trying to verbalize the solution. Have students write down the solution and check it carefully before explaining.

Getting Started:

Students will probably find that a series of pictures will help them keep track of the steps. Moving scraps of paper labeled chicken, fox, corn will help simulate the situation.

Which two things can be left together, if any?

Must the woman always carry something in the boat?

Can she take something back with her?

Solution:

Let *Ch, F,* and *C* represent the chicken, fox, and corn. The arrow indicates the direction in which the woman is rowing across the river.

There are two solutions.

F, C	Ch→			F, C	Ch→	
F, C	←	Ch		F, C	←	Ch
C	F→	Ch		F	C →	Ch
C	←Ch	F		F	←Ch	C
Ch	C→	F	or	Ch	F →	C
Ch	←	F, C		Ch	←	F, C
	Ch→	F, C			Ch→	F, C
		F, Ch, C				F, Ch, C

Going Beyond:

1. Is it easier to explain the solution when looking at notes? (Seven steps are difficult to keep clear in your head when explaining the problem.)

2. This problem shows the value of careful recording when many steps are involved.

11. PLANE LOGIC

Last Tuesday on flight #196 to Denver, Mrs. Jones, Miss Smith, and Mr. Bond were seated together in row 13. At one particular time, all of the following were true:

A. Mrs. Jones had her traytable down.

B. The person sitting in the window seat was to the left of the other two.

C. Mr. Bond was sitting next to Mrs. Jones.

D. The lady in the center was reading a magazine.

E. Miss Smith was reading a book.

F. Miss Smith was the stepdaughter of the person on Mr. Bond's left.

Who was sitting in the aisle seat?

11. PLANE LOGIC

Answer: Mr. Bond

About the Problem:

This is a fairly easy logic problem. With most students, this kind of problem needs to be read carefully two or three times. No time pressure should be placed on beginning problem solvers working this problem. If some students get answers quickly, accepting them could intimidate others or further convince some students that they are not good problem solvers. It may be best to assign this problem near the end of the period to make sure students can think through it at their own speed.

The problem contains extraneous information to see if the solver can differentiate between what is and isn't important to the solution of the problem.

Getting Started:

Read through the problem carefully a couple of times before you try to start drawing conclusions.

Take notes or draw pictures to help clarify what you know.

Once you think you have the answer, go back and check it with each statement to be sure it's right.

Solution:

We can analyze the statements in this problem in order.

A. Not helpful.
B. Tells us they were sitting on the left side of the airplane.
C. We can conclude from this that Jones or Bond is sitting in the center seat.
D. This tells us one of the ladies was sitting in the center. Combine this with C, and we know that Mrs. Jones is sitting in the center.
E. Not helpful, but gives further confirmation that Mrs. Jones is sitting in the center.
F. If Mr. Bond were sitting in the window seat on the left side of the plane, no one could be on his left. Therefore, Mr. Bond could not be sitting in the window seat. He must be sitting in an aisle seat.

Going Beyond:

1. Was every statement helpful? (No.)

2. Which *extraneous* statements could have been omitted without changing the problem? (A and E)

3. Do we need all four of the other statements or could we have solved the problem with only three clues? (It can be solved without clue C.)

12. BRETT'S AGE

Brett's father is four times as old as Brett is now. In four years, Brett's age will be one-third of his father's age. How old are they now?

12. BRETT'S AGE

Answer: Brett is 8 years old and his father is 32.

About the Problem:

No algebra is needed to solve this problem. Just some common sense combined with trial and error will lead to a solution. The trial and error is very minimal with a little thinking about the logical bounds of Brett's age.

Getting Started:

Would it make sense for Brett to be 4 years old now?

Would it make sense for Brett to be 25 now?

Make a chart to test possible ages. Include ages now and in 4 years.

Make the present ratio 4 times. Look for a future ratio of 3 times.

Solution:

If we start our list at 5 years for Brett's age now, we find the solution quickly.

Now			In 4 years	
Brett	Father		Brett	Father
5	$4 \times 5 = 20$		9	$24 \neq 3 \times 9$
6	$4 \times 6 = 24$		10	$28 \neq 3 \times 10$
7	$4 \times 7 = 28$		11	$32 \neq 3 \times 11$, but close!
8	$4 \times 8 = 32$		12	$36 = 3 \times 12$, Answer!

Thus, Brett is now 8 years old and his father is 32.

Going Beyond:

When will Brett be half his father's age? (When he is 24.)

Show students how they could jump by ten-year periods to see when the ratio starts getting close to one-half.

Brett	Father	
8	32	$8 < \frac{1}{2} \times 32$
18	42	$18 < \frac{1}{2} \times 42$
28	52	$28 > \frac{1}{2} \times 52$

The correct age must be between 18 and 28.

Ferdinand has a three-liter unmarked container, a five-liter unmarked container, and an unlimited supply of root beer. How can he use them to measure out four liters of root beer?

GUZZLE
BLUB
SLURP
S-S-S-SLURP

3.7853L

Answer: There are many possible correct answers. Two are shown in the Solution section.

About the Problem:

This problem demands some exploration and imagination on the part of the problem solver. One suspects that a combination of filling and exchanges between two containers will give the desired result. The biggest problem here may be trying to diagram a situation that helps to visualize what is happening.

If possible, bring in two containers, a water source, and a bucket to demonstrate the answer once the students have solved the problem.

Getting Started:

Is it okay to pour from one container to the other?

Can you fill one of the containers with two liters?

Make a chart or diagram of each step.

Solution:

It takes six steps to obtain four liters in the 5-liter container. The solution can also be reached in eight steps by filling the 3-liter container first. Any solution should be accepted, but the shortest procedure is preferable.

Here is the six-step solution.

5-liter   3-liter
Container   Container

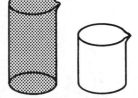

Step 1. Fill the 5-liter container.

Step 2. Pour 3 liters into the 3-liter container from the 5-liter container. This leaves 2 liters in the larger container.

Step 3. Empty the 3-liter container.

Step 4. Pour the 2 liters into the 3-liter container.

Step 5. Fill the 5-liter container.

Step 6. Fill the 3-liter container from the 5-liter container. Four liters are left!

Here is the eight-step solution.

Step 1. Fill the 3-liter container.
Step 2. Pour 3 liters into the 5-liter container.
Step 3. Fill the 3-liter container again.
Step 4. Pour 3 liters into the 5-liter container, leaving 1 liter in the 3-liter container.
Step 5. Empty the 5-liter container.
Step 6. Pour 1 liter from the 3-liter container into the 5-liter container.
Step 7. Fill the 3-liter container.
Step 8. Pour 3 liters into the 5-liter container to have a total of 4 liters in the larger container.

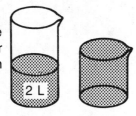

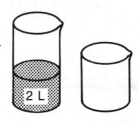

12. FOOL'S GOLD

A jeweler has four small bars that are supposed to be gold. He knows that one is counterfeit. The counterfeit bar has a slightly different weight than a real gold bar. Using only a balance scale, how can the jeweler find the counterfeit bar?

12. FOOL'S GOLD

Answer: See the Solution section.

About the Problem:

This problem may require some careful thought and note-taking before the deductive logic can be explained.

It may be necessary to explain that a balance scale only shows whether the amounts on either side of the scale are equal and, if not, which is lighter and which heavier.

Have *each* student *write out* the solution. When one student verbalizes a solution for the entire class, many students may not work the problem, knowing the odds are good they will not be called upon for the answer.

Getting Started:

Does the problem tell whether the counterfeit is heavier or lighter?

Try to account for all possible outcomes.

Solution:

One solution is given below. A different solution would involve weighing all pairs and comparing the combinations. Either solution is acceptable.

Step 1. Pick any two bars and put one on each side of the scale.

Step 2. a. If they *balance,* the two weighed were both good bars.

b. If they *don't balance,* the two *not* weighed are both good bars.

Step 3. Place the two good bars on one side of the scale and the other two on the other side.

Step 4. a. If the two good bars are heavier, the counterfeit bar must be lighter.

b. If the two good bars are lighter, the counterfeit bar must be heavier.

Step 5. Separate and weigh the two that include the counterfeit bar and locate the counterfeit.

Going Beyond:

1. A second way to solve this problem is to weigh all possible pairs of bars until an imbalance is found. Which of the two procedures would be best if there was one counterfeit bar in 64 bars?

2. How would you proceed with 64 bars? (Follow a procedure similar to the five-step procedure above, except start by weighing two sets of 16 bars.)

13. FOUR WEIGHTS

Using a balance scale, you must be able to balance every whole kilogram amount from 1 kg through 15 kg. You may choose four standard weights to use, each a different number of kilograms. Which weights should you choose?

13. FOUR WEIGHTS

Answer: 1 kg, 2 kg, 4 kg, and 8 kg

About the Problem:

This problem was designed to serve as a helpful warm-up to *Chain Reaction.* It is also a good problem for beginning problem solvers. Its solution is related to base 2, but understanding of base 2 is not a prerequisite for the solution. Students can simply think of these numbers as doubles.

Getting Started:

What amounts must you be able to weigh with the four weights you choose?

What is the smallest amount to weigh?

The next smallest amount?

What two ways could you weigh two kilograms?

Solution:

By starting with the smallest amount to be weighed, students can find the solution using trial and error. Here are the ways that amounts from 1 kg through 15 kg could be weighed using 1 kg, 2 kg, 4 kg, and 8 kg.

$1 = 1$
$2 = 2$
$3 = 1 + 2$
$4 = 4$
$5 = 1 + 4$
$6 = 2 + 4$
$7 = 1 + 2 + 4$
$8 = 8$
$9 = 1 + 8$
$10 = 2 + 8$
$11 = 1 + 2 + 8$
$12 = 4 + 8$
$13 = 1 + 4 + 8$
$14 = 2 + 4 + 8$
$15 = 1 + 2 + 4 + 8$

Going Beyond:

1. What is the relationship among the numbers 1, 2, 4, and 8? (All are powers of two, or each is the double of the preceding number.)

2. Suppose you wanted to balance every whole kilogram amount from 1 kg through 31 kg. Which five weights should you choose? (1 kg, 2 kg, 4 kg, 8 kg, 16 kg)

How can a chain with 63 links be cut in three places so that you could hand a person *any* number of links from 1 to 63? (A cut link is still counted as a link.)

13. CHAIN REACTION

Answer: See the Solution section.

About the Problem:

The note that a cut link is considered a link is important. Also, some students might ask if the original chain is connected to itself, making a closed loop. It is not.

The *Warm-up* for this problem will be a definite help. If your class is above average or gifted, you may want to give this problem without having solved the *Warm-up* problem.

Getting Started:

When you make the first cut, how many pieces do you have?

Can you change the problem to an easier problem?

Solution:

The fewest numbers which can be combined to total any number from 1 to 63 are the doubles, or powers of 2, starting from 1: 1, 2, 4, 8, 16, 32.

Desired weight	Combination
1	1
2	2
3	1 + 2
4	4
5	1 + 4
6	2 + 4
7	1 + 2 + 4
•	•
•	•
•	•
21	16 + 4 + 1
22	16 + 4 + 2
23	16 + 4 + 2 + 1
24	16 + 8
25	16 + 8 + 1
•	•
•	•
•	•
61	32 + 16 + 8 + 4 + 1
62	32 + 16 + 8 + 4 + 2
63	32 + 16 + 8 + 4 + 2 + 1

Knowing this, the numbers above give us some target numbers. Starting at the upper end, we want a 32, so we cut the 33rd link.

We have two of the desired numbers, 1 and 32, so next we try to cut a 16.

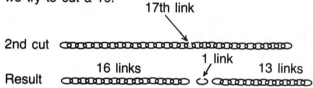

We now have a 32, a 16, a 1, and a 2 (two ones), so we try to cut an 8.

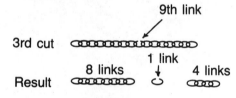

This gives us the 8 and 4 we wanted, as well as an additional 1. We have all we need to make any combination of 1 through 63 in three cuts.

Going Beyond:

1. What was the key to the problem? (Discovering or knowing that the numbers needed were 1, 2, 4, 8, 16, and 32.)

2. How do these numbers relate to base 2? (They represent the place value positions: 2^0, 2^1, 2^2, 2^3, 2^4 and 2^5.)

13. IT'S MAGIC

If you know how to use the "magic cards" below, you can ask a friend to think of a secret number between 1 and 31. Then ask your friend to answer "yes" or "no" to each of the following questions: "Is the secret number on card #1? On #2? On #3? On #4? On #5?" After your friend has answered each question, you can say what the secret number is. Before you learn the "magic trick," can you figure it out?

1	3	5	7
9	11	13	15
17	19	21	23
25	27	29	31

card #1

2	3	6	7
10	11	14	15
18	19	22	23
26	27	30	31

card #2

4	5	6	7
12	13	14	15
20	21	22	23
28	29	30	31

card #3

8	9	10	11
12	13	14	15
24	25	26	27
28	29	30	31

card #4

16	17	18	19
20	21	22	23
24	25	26	27
28	29	30	31

card #5

13. IT'S MAGIC

Answer: See the Solution section.

About the Problem:

The problem is closely related to *Chain Reaction* and its *Warm-up.* If students have solved those problems, this one may be easy for them. A knowledge of base 2 will make this problem simpler. It may be a good way to introduce base 2.

One way to introduce students to the problem is to give all students a copy of the problem as it is written above. Another approach is to make the cards and present the problem as a "magic trick" or puzzle to the entire class. An alternative is to share the secret with one or two students from the class. Let them prepare the cards and make the presentation. This can be a very enjoyable problem for the students because it seems like the presenter is "reading minds."

Getting Started:

There are patterns on the cards that may give some clues to finding their secret. These patterns are not too obvious. Some clues are given below. Successive clues are more helpful.

Look for patterns on the cards.

Which number or numbers appear on every card?

Which numbers appear on only one card?

What is special about the numbers that appear on a card only once?

Can you add combinations of these special numbers to total any of the numbers?

Solution:

The number a student is thinking of is the sum of each of the numbers in the upper left corner of each card the number is on. For example, the number 10 is on cards 2 and 4. The numbers in the upper left corner of cards 2 and 4 are 2 and 8 ($2 + 8 = 10$).

The basis for this puzzle is the number base 2. If numbers are written in base 2, the place value positions starting from the right are $2^0 = 1$, $2^1 = 2$, $2^2 = 4$, $2^3 = 8$, $2^4 = 16$, and so on. For example, the number 9 in base 2 is written 1001_{two}.

8	4	2	1
1	0	0	1

All numbers that have a 1 in the ones place in base 2 are on card 1. All numbers that have a 1 in the twos place are on card 2, in the fours place on card 3, in the eights place on card 4, and finally in the sixteens place on card 5.

A complete listing of the first 31 counting numbers written in base two is shown below.

	16	8	4	2	1
1					1
2				1	0
3				1	1
4			1	0	0
5			1	0	1
6			1	1	0
7			1	1	1
8		1	0	0	0
9		1	0	0	1
10		1	0	1	0
11		1	0	1	1
12		1	1	0	0
13		1	1	0	1
14		1	1	1	0
15		1	1	1	1
16	1	0	0	0	0
17	1	0	0	0	1
18	1	0	0	1	0
19	1	0	0	1	1
20	1	0	1	0	0
21	1	0	1	0	1
22	1	0	1	1	0
23	1	0	1	1	1
24	1	1	0	0	0
25	1	1	0	0	1
26	1	1	0	1	0
27	1	1	0	1	1
28	1	1	1	0	0
29	1	1	1	0	1
30	1	1	1	1	0
31	1	1	1	1	1

Going Beyond:

Point out to students that base 2 is used in representing information in most computers. The ones and zeros are sometimes represented electrically by power "on" and power "off."

14. FAST DRAW

Form exactly two squares by drawing five lines.
By drawing six lines. By drawing seven lines.

14. FAST DRAW

Answers: See the Solution section.

About the Problem:

This problem is designed to have students think about results of diagramming. There may be some ambiguity in the problem, but that may let students be innovative and imaginative, which is the purpose of this problem.

Getting Started:

Think of ways two squares can be drawn.

Can the squares share a line? Two lines?

Draw two squares and think backwards how they might be created.

Solution:

This is a place to accept various approaches to the problem. Accept any answer the student can justify. Three solutions are given here.

5 lines

6 lines

7 lines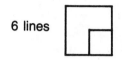

Going Beyond:

1. Can you draw two equilateral triangles using four lines?

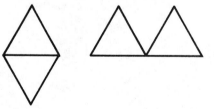

2. Can you draw two equilateral triangles using five lines? (two solutions)

What is the greatest number of pieces you can cut a cake into by making four straight cuts with a knife? Each cut must pass through the top and bottom of the cake.

Answer: 11 pieces

About the Problem:

A potential stumbling block with this problem is visualizing the cuts. Chords and a circle can be used to model the problem.

Getting Started:

What is the maximum number of pieces with one cut? With two? With three?

Do you get more or fewer pieces by cutting through an intersection?

Solution:

The first cut gives two pieces.

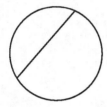

The second cut adds two more pieces.

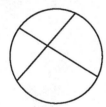

The third cut adds three pieces as shown below.

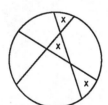

3 new pieces

The fourth cut adds four new pieces.

The results can be summarized in a table.

Number of Cuts	Maximum number of pieces
1	2
2	4
3	7
4	11

Going Beyond:

1. What pattern might give a clue to the answer for the maximum number of pieces produced by five cuts? (The difference pattern between pieces is a difference of 2, then 3, then 4, then 5, and so on.)

2. What if all the cuts need not pass through the top and bottom of the cake? Explore this more difficult problem, which can be summarized in this table:

Number of Cuts	Maximum number of pieces
1	2
2	4
3	8
4	15

14. SQUARE SHARE

Lines can divide squares into smaller squares. The table below shows the number of lines required to divide a square into a certain number of smaller squares. Can you see a pattern that would tell you how many lines would be required to divide a square into 100 smaller squares? Into 400 smaller squares? Into n smaller squares?

Number of smaller squares	Number of lines
4	2
9	4
16	6
25	8
36	10
•	
•	
•	
100	
400	
n	

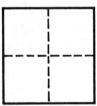

2 lines
4 smaller squares

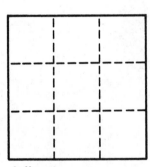

4 lines
9 smaller squares

14. SQUARE SHARE

Answers: For 100 squares, 18 lines.
For 400 squares, 38 lines.
For n squares, $2(\sqrt{n} - 1)$.

About the Problem:

Students attempting this problem should have solved several problems involving tables. They should be conscious of relationships and patterns.

Getting Started:

Look for patterns in each column of the table.

How are 6 and 16 related? 8 and 25? 10 and 36?

How many lines are required on *one side* of a square to make three sections? Four sections?

Solution:

Since two lines on one side of a square make three sections, four lines make 3^2 or 9 smaller squares. Since three lines on one side of a square make four sections, six lines make 4^2 or 16 smaller squares.

In order to make 100 smaller squares, we need $\sqrt{100} = 10$ sections along each side, and hence we need $10 - 1 = 9$ lines along each side of the square. So $2 \times 9 = 18$ lines will make 100 smaller squares.

To make 400 smaller squares, we need $\sqrt{400} = 20$ sections along each side of the square, and hence we need $20 - 1 = 19$ lines along each side. So $2 \times 19 = 38$ lines will make 400 smaller squares.

Similarly, the number of lines required to make n squares is $2 \times (\sqrt{n} - 1)$.

Going Beyond:

Three lines can divide an equilateral triangle into four smaller equilateral triangles as shown below.

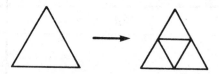

How many lines divide an equilateral triangle into nine smaller triangles? (6 lines) Into 25 smaller triangles? (12 lines)

15. PRIME TIME

A *prime number* is a number that has no factors except for one and itself. Can you list the first ten prime numbers? (The number one is not considered a prime number.)

15. PRIME TIME

Answer: 2, 3, 5, 7, 11, 13, 17, 19, 23, 29

About the Problem:

Students may already be familiar with prime numbers. If so, they may wish to start right in on *Goldbach's Conjecture.* If students have not had much work with primes, this warm-up problem may be necessary to have success with *Goldbach's Conjecture* and its *Extension.*

Students may wonder why the number one is not considered a prime. After solving problem *15. Extension,* they will see why one is not considered a prime.

Getting Started:

Try dividing each number by other numbers.

Why is there only one even prime? What is it?

Solution:

Most students will solve this by simply testing each number to see if it is divisible by any smaller number.

Going Beyond:

1. What are the second ten prime numbers? (31, 37, 41, 43, 47, 53, 59, 61, 67, and 71)
2. What is a composite number? (A number that has factors other than itself and one.)
3. What one counting number is neither prime nor composite? (1)

It is believed that every even number greater than four can be expressed as the sum of two primes.

Examples: $68 = 7 + 61$
$12 = 5 + 7$

Can you find sums for all of the two-digit even numbers?

89

How about 61 + 7 ?

Answer: See the sample answers in the Solution section.

About the Problem:

The problem can add a puzzle or discovery element to some basic factoring practice. The reason that this is a "conjecture" is that there is no mathematical *proof* that it is true. (A statement must be provable to be considered a *fact*.) Point out that if one example were found as an exception, then it would no longer be a "conjecture."

The *Warm-up* problem should provide students with the background information on primes needed to solve this problem.

A list of the primes less than 100 is useful in this solution.

Getting Started:

Is 1 considered a prime? (No)

What is a prime number?

Did the problem say that there was only one sum for each number?

Can you find a number that has more than one solution?

Solution:

Trial and error is the main strategy here. A list of sample solutions are shown below.

$20 = 3 + 17$	$60 = 19 + 41$
$22 = 5 + 17$	$62 = 19 + 43$
$24 = 5 + 19$	$64 = 23 + 41$
$26 = 3 + 23$	$66 = 23 + 43$
$28 = 11 + 17$	$68 = 7 + 61$
$30 = 7 + 23$	$70 = 11 + 59$
$32 = 3 + 29$	$72 = 13 + 59$
$34 = 3 + 31$	$74 = 13 + 61$
$36 = 5 + 31$	$76 = 17 + 59$
$38 = 7 + 31$	$78 = 17 + 61$
$40 = 11 + 29$	$80 = 19 + 61$
$42 = 13 + 29$	$82 = 59 + 23$
$44 = 3 + 41$	$84 = 17 + 67$
$46 = 3 + 43$	$86 = 19 + 67$
$48 = 5 + 43$	$88 = 17 + 71$
$50 = 19 + 31$	$90 = 19 + 71$
$52 = 5 + 47$	$92 = 19 + 73$
$54 = 7 + 47$	$94 = 23 + 71$
$56 = 13 + 43$	$96 = 23 + 73$
$58 = 17 + 41$	$98 = 37 + 61$

Going Beyond:

1. Why is the prime number two never used in any of the sums in this problem? (It is the only even prime. The sum of two and any other prime would be the sum of an even and an odd number, which would be odd.)

2. Pick five consecutive even three-digit numbers. Find pairs of primes whose sum is each of these five numbers.

15. FUNDAMENTAL THEOREM

The Fundamental Theorem of Arithmetic states that every natural number can be expressed as the product of prime numbers in only one way. Find the prime factorizations of 357 and 10,780.

15. FUNDAMENTAL THEOREM

Answer: $357 = 3 \times 7 \times 17$
$10{,}780 = 2 \times 2 \times 5 \times 7 \times 7 \times 11$

About the Problem:

This is an important concept for sixth and seventh graders studying primes, composites, least common multiples, and greatest common factors.

Students learn to "chop away" at factoring a large number by trying division by smaller primes. It is helpful to know that in testing a number they only need to divide by all primes less than the square root of the number. That is, when testing for factors of 101, it is only necessary to test primes up to 10 (the approximate square root of 101). Knowing tests for divisibility for 2, 3, 4, 5, 6, 9, and 10 is also very helpful.

Getting Started:

Try dividing the numbers by some small primes.

Double check each factor to be sure it is prime.

Solution:

"Factor tree" solutions are shown below.

$357 = 3 \times 7 \times 17$

$10{,}780 = 2 \times 2 \times 5 \times 7 \times 7 \times 11 = 2^2 \times 5 \times 7^2 \times 11$

Going Beyond:

There are three prime factors of 357. There are six prime factors of 10,780. If the number one were considered a prime number, then the fundamental theorem of arithmetic could not state that there is an exact (unique) number of prime factors for each number. For instance, the number 357 could be factored as $1 \times 3 \times 7 \times 17$ or $1 \times 1 \times 1 \times 3 \times 7 \times 17$.

16. ROLL-A-SUM

Roll a pair of dice 36 times. Record the sums. Which sum appeared most often? Which sum appeared least often? Do you think the chances are the same for rolling any sum from 2 through 12? Why?

16. ROLL-A-SUM

Answer: Answers will vary.

About the Problem:

Dice serve as a good model for developing an understanding of beginning probabilities. This problem provides students an opportunity to collect data and then make an inference based on the data. The model is a simple one that students can easily understand.

If a small group or entire class participate in this problem, the *combined data* should provide a more realistic model of what is expected to happen. A discussion of the data should lead into problem 16. *Tumblers.*

Getting Started:

It may be interesting to let students organize their data collection as they like. After the problem is solved, take a few minutes to discuss the value of a table, tally marks, and other recording methods.

Solution:

No two students will get exactly the same result. It is even possible that a student would roll one number 36 times (one chance in 6^{36} or about one chance in 10,000,000,000,000,000,000,000,000,000).

Seven is most likely to appear more often than the other numbers. Two and twelve are least likely to appear. The chances for rolling numbers are not the same. There are more combinations of the dice that make certain numbers compared to other numbers. This problem leads right into finding the chances of each number coming up, as developed in *Tumblers.*

16. TUMBLERS

A pair of regular dice, one white and one red, are rolled. Make a list of all the combinations that could come up. For each possible sum, what are the chances that the sum will be rolled?

Red die	White die	Sum
1	1	2
1	2	3
1	3	
1	4	
1	5	
1	6	
2	1	3
2	2	4
2	3	
2		
2		
2		
3	1	
3		
3		
3		
3		
3		

Red die	White die	Sum
4		
4		
4		
4		
4		
4		
5		
6	6	12

Answer: See the table in the Solution section.

About the Problem:

This problem is another example of organized listing which gives all the permutations of two dice.

It may be necessary to explain the table carefully to the students and to lead them through the first few answers. Once they see the pattern, they shouldn't have any trouble.

Getting Started:

If one die lands with a one up, how many different numbers could land up on the second die?

Fill in the first two columns in the table to give every possibility that could occur.

Add the numbers in the first two columns to find the sum.

How many different combinations will there be all together?

Solution:

There are 36 different ways that pairs of numbers can be rolled. The sum of eight appears 5 times. So the chances an eight will come up are 5 out of 36 or 5/36. Seven is the most common sum. It appears 6 times (1 + 6, 2 + 5, 3 + 4, 4 + 3, 5 + 2, 6 + 1). So the chances a seven will come up are 6/36 or 1/6. A summary is given below:

Sum	Times occuring	Chance of rolling
2	1	1/36
3	2	2/36 or 1/18
4	3	3/36 or 1/12
5	4	4/36 or 1/9
6	5	5/36
7	6	6/36 or 1/6
8	5	5/36
9	4	4/36 or 1/9
10	3	3/36 or 1/12
11	2	2/36 or 1/18
12	1	1/36

Going Beyond:

1. Which numbers are least likely to appear? (2 and 12) Why? (Because there are fewer sums that total 2 and 12.)

2. Because the number 7 is most likely to appear more than any other number, does that mean that it always will? (No.)

16. DICE THRICE

Rolling three regular dice, what is the smallest sum that could be rolled? What is the largest sum? How many different ways could a sum of ten be rolled?

16. DICE THRICE

Answers: Smallest sum is 3.
Largest sum is 18.
A sum of 10 can be rolled in 27 ways.

About the Problem:

This extension of *Tumblers* will provide students an opportunity to see if they can make an organized list of the permutations of three dice that total ten.

It may be necessary to clarify that the sum 6 + 3 + 1 occurs with different combinations of the three dice.

Getting Started:

It may help to think of the three dice as red, white, and blue to make sure you count all possible sums.

Make an organized table or list.

Solution:

The smallest sum that can be rolled is 3 (1, 1, 1). The largest number that can be rolled is 18 (6, 6, 6). A 10 can be rolled in 27 different ways as shown below.

(6, 3, 1)	(5, 4, 1)	(4, 5, 1)
(6, 2, 2)	(5, 3, 2)	(4, 4, 2)
(6, 1, 3)	(5, 2, 3)	(4, 3, 3)
	(5, 1, 4)	(4, 2, 4)
		(4, 1, 5)

(3, 6, 1)	(2, 6, 2)	(1, 6, 3)
(3, 5, 2)	(2, 5, 3)	(1, 5, 4)
(3, 4, 3)	(2, 4, 4)	(1, 4, 5)
(3, 3, 4)	(2, 3, 5)	(1, 3, 6)
(3, 2, 5)	(2, 2, 6)	
(3, 1, 6)		

Going Beyond:

1. If you throw three dice at once, how many different ways could they land? (There are six ways the first die could land, six ways the second could land and six ways the third could land. So there are 6 × 6 × 6 = 216 ways.)

2. What are the chances of rolling a three with three dice? (1 out of 6^3 or 1/216)

3. What are the chances of rolling a 24 with 4 dice? (1 out of 6^4 or 1/1296)

2. MAGIC SQUARE
(Continued from page 12)

We see that 5 *must* be in the center, since it is the only number that is used four times. It is nice that our distribution chart shows four numbers used two times and four numbers used three times. This is just what we wanted to have happen from our previous position analysis. The numbers 2, 4, 6, and 8 must be in the corners. The numbers 1, 3, 7, and 9 must be in the outside center positions. We can fill in the numbers with some checking of sums. The unique answer is

2	7	6
9	5	1
4	3	8

Rotations and/or reflections of this answer are not considered different answers.

Going Beyond:

It is a worthwhile experience to work through the solution to this problem with the entire class. The strategies and reasoning are more important than the solution. If you do try the class approach, give the same problem to the students once or twice later in the year. This is not the kind of solution approach that is memorized. The solution should help develop students' reasoning abilities.

9. PAINTOMINOES
(Continued from page 52)

3. Use the 12 pentomino shapes as puzzle pieces.
    a. Use any 3 pieces to form a 3 by 5 rectangle.
    b. Use any 4 pieces to form a 4 by 5 rectangle.
    c. Use any 5 pieces to form a square.
    d. Use any 6 pieces to form a 5 by 6 rectangle.
    e. Use all 12 pieces to form a 6 by 10 rectangle.
       (This is a very difficult puzzle.)
    Sample answers:

a.
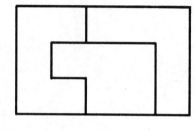

b.
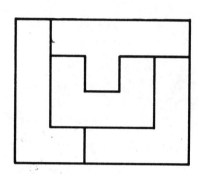

c.
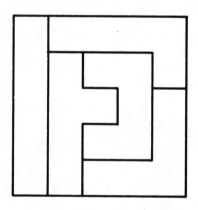

d.
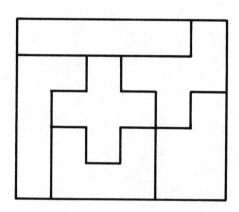

e.
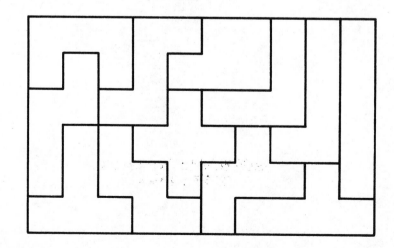